Praise for *Pla...*

"This book fills an importa...   ...s of physics to making change   ...thoughts about how we use our energy ...particularly important. Bravo!"

— M. J. Ryan, author of *The Happiness Makeover*

"Brenda Anderson's groundbreaking new book addresses our interdependent business world and personal lives and the choices that shape them. It is full of practical examples plucked from our everyday work environment. Although we can't change everything that happens to us on a given day, with Brenda's help we can learn to ride the waves of change toward our ultimate goals. This book will help every reader find new ways to accomplish more, each and every day."

— Roger Dow, president and CEO, Travel Industry Association of America

"*Playing the Quantum Field* is a must-read for all adults. As Anderson points out, the plain and simple truth is that if we're willing to explore life by looking through a different (and better) prism, we'll have more satisfaction, fulfillment, and happiness in our lives. Easy and fun to read, the book offers new insights and advice on many issues we all face in our day-to-day lives. In fact, it could change your entire life, improving your approach to professional and personal relationships."

— Ray Marcy, executive chairperson, NurseFinders, Inc.

"Have you ever wondered how you will find the energy and creativity to address the future challenges of your fast-changing industry? Have you noticed that solutions that once worked are, in a strange way, no longer effective? Brenda Anderson gives *what-the-bleep?* reality a practical purpose, and her book puts each individual into the driver's seat of their own destiny. *Playing the Quantum Field* bridges the old and new ways of thinking, offering sometimes hilarious examples of how the old and new approaches work — or don't work — in real life. She demonstrates that many of us are already using these ideas intuitively, and effectively!"

— Gabriele Hilberg, PhD,
psychotherapist and business consultant

PLAYING
the Quantum
FIELD

PLAYING
the Quantum
FIELD

How Changing Your Choices
Can Change Your Life

Brenda Anderson

New World Library
Novato, California

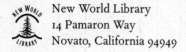

New World Library
14 Pamaron Way
Novato, California 94949

The author's stories used as examples throughout this book are true, although identifying details such as name and location have been changed to protect the privacy of those involved.

Text design and typography by Tona Pearce Myers

ISBN-10: 1-57731-527-8
ISBN-13: 978-1-57731-527-8
Printed in the United States

To my mom, Jean

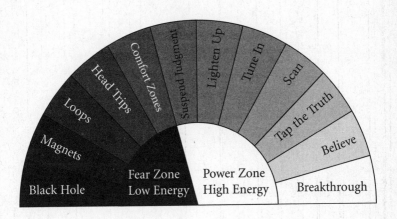

PART ONE

THE TEN ENERGETIC CHOICES THAT SHAPE OUR LIVES

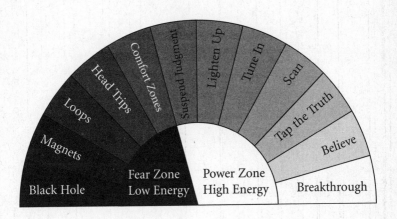

Black Hole

Magnets

Loops

Head Trips

Comfort Zones

Suspend Judgment

Lighten Up

Tune In

Scan

Tap the Truth

Believe

Breakthrough

Fear Zone
Low Energy

Power Zone
High Energy

CHAPTER ONE

THE FIELD

Have you ever experienced a sudden breakthrough? You know that feeling, when what you picture in your head actually happens and you want to pinch yourself because you can't believe it's real? Or when you have one of those moments of clarity, and your biggest problem suddenly disappears because you look at it differently, or when the perfect solution presents itself out of the blue? That's when you're playing the quantum field.

When I was an undergraduate, I had a particularly wonderful experience of playing the Field. During my last two years of college I had the good fortune to study abroad in England and Germany. As it was for many young people at that time, hitchhiking was my main mode of transportation outside the cities. During one semester break my friend Mary and I decided to visit the Lake District, north of London. We caught rides on the M-5, a major highway, and found ourselves on a small country road later in the day than we'd hoped.

We walked for hours in the rain and fog, and the few cars that passed by didn't stop. Darkness began to settle in. We couldn't see twenty feet in front of us and felt scared. I had learned from severe asthma attacks in early childhood that if I focused on my fear I would only feel even more desperate than I already was. I told Mary this, and we agreed to put our fear aside. We both let out a sigh. As we continued walking, we talked about how much fun we were having exploring Europe and immediately felt better. We told ourselves we'd find a ride and would be safe.

The fog was settling in about ten minutes later, when out of nowhere two headlights emerged. Timothy, an elderly Englishman around fifty (well, that looked "elderly" then!) drove up in his camper and rolled down his window. "Have you two ladies lost your way?" he asked kindly. We admitted we had. He said he was on holiday and didn't generally drive this way, and didn't know why he had turned down that particular road, but was glad he had. Then he took us to a campground and made dinner while we dried off and warmed ourselves by the fire. That night he slept in the cab and let us sleep in his camper.

Instead of letting fear dominate our thoughts and actions, sending us into panic and ineffectiveness, Mary and I chose to connect to the power of the Field by making our intentions very clear. Timothy's appearance that cold, rainy night might seem like luck or coincidence, but what exactly does that mean? Even Timothy had said he didn't understand why he had turned down that road. When your intention is clear, the Field quickly starts pulling things together. Some people call this synchronicity. I call it playing the quantum field.

Why can't we create these magical outcomes all the time? Now, more than ever, we need the ability to create breakthrough results at will. The world is changing, and we need some new operating instructions. Life continues to accelerate, and we find ourselves at a new frontier as we realize our world is filled with more change, more danger, and less integrity than we'd ever thought possible. We're overstimulated and maxed out. Something's got to give.

And it has. In a way you may not have imagined.

Science is on the verge of proving that everything is dynamic and connected. What was once considered the New Age fringe thinking of renegade physicists has been embraced by more and more people as a probability. This new worldview is reflected in key scientific discoveries, kicked off by Einstein a century ago, and is becoming so widely accepted that it was celebrated by the World Year of Physics in 2005. The quantum field is showing itself up close and personal for increasing numbers of us. Look at how awareness of the Field is expressing itself in our culture: the vernacular of personal-growth classes and spiritual practices help people "ground" and "get centered." TV audiences are fascinated with the numerous shows about kids and adults tapping into special powers. Advertising for cellular phone services promise to help us "get connected," and the Internet itself is a metaphor for the interconnected web that more and more people are experiencing.

Even the practice of law is reflecting this connection. In South Africa, Nelson Mandela supports the Promotion of National Unity and Reconciliation Act of 1995. This "truth and reconciliation process" is based on *ubuntu*, a Zulu or Xhosa word that means "humanity to others." If you keep hurting the people who hurt you, the situation will never end. We are all connected. In medicine, more and more holistic health practices are acknowledging that the body is not separate from the mind and spirit. They all work together. Major global economic powers are realizing they cannot ignore the plight of entire nations because of the interconnectedness of all nations and the consequent effects on the stock market. In addition, world religions that have traditionally been closed to other perspectives are reaching out to each other to explore a connecting reality they can all respect and honor. Nondenominational churches are thriving.

These provocative glimpses into different areas of life are imperfect metaphors for what much of the world is beginning to recognize: that there is a larger reality out there than we have ever imagined. We are on the brink of a huge shift in awareness that will absolutely change how we live.

In plain English, every person and every thing is operating in a single energy field, and we each have much more power to create our lives than we ever imagined. According to Merriam-Webster, a *field* is a "region or space in which a given effect exists." You've probably heard of magnetic fields, like those around your microwave. Or you may have felt the fields of sacred places like the pyramids, Stonehenge, and the Holy Land. People have personal fields. Have you ever noticed how some people feel warm and inviting, while others seem to radiate a kind of "stay away" energy? Even though you experience the Field in small glimpses and in different areas of life, the epiphany for most of us is that these glimpses are all connected and part of the same field. Imagine it as one big grid that everything is a part of. No one is "off the grid," even if they think they are or want to be.

In the old thinking, the cab you take to the airport is one field. The plane you take to your destination is another. That kind of thinking limits us. In the new thinking, the cab, the plane, the sky, and the universe are all one Field. The power of the Field is that you can tap into this collective. And the better equipped we become at embracing this new worldview, the more we will be able to usher in this new way of living.

What we are really talking about with the quantum field is possibility. Think of the quantum field as all possibility and potential, which you can consciously access — if you know how. Anyone who studies quantum physics knows that your thoughts connect you to this field of possibility. In the words of noted physicist Fred Alan Wolf, "Reality depends upon our choices of what and how we choose to observe. These choices, in turn, depend upon our minds or, more specifically, the content of our thoughts."[1] For the purpose of this book, I am going to focus on your choices so that you can discover the quantum field of possibility organically for yourself. I will translate this concept into simple language and day-to-day examples you can learn and practice so that by the end of this book, you will have experienced first-hand the power of the quantum field.

THE AGE OF ACCOUNTABILITY

A lot of emphasis is put on personal accountability today. Upheavals in religion, politics, business, and culture are demanding that we take more responsibility for the choices we make and the results we create. Now that lifetime employment with one company is no longer the norm, we've taken responsibility for our careers. With changes in medical care and insurance, we've had to become responsible for our health. Because we can't count on Social Security benefits, we've assumed responsibility for our retirement.

It's time to expand this sense of accountability into every moment and every choice we make. By playing the Field, it is possible to become more accountable for our decisions. Although none of us want to be slaves to any system or person, we still end up enslaving ourselves with some of our thinking and actions. We no longer want to feel as if we're powerless to affect our lives. And we will realize we won't be powerless if we learn to play.

Playing the Field is the responsible way to live and to use your energy. When you choose not to tap the Field, you more easily feel like a victim, forgetting that your choices have power. In the past, when we have tapped the quantum field, we've sometimes performed miracles, persuading masses of people to change their minds, or loving a teen back into the fold. At other times we've chosen manipulation or control — choices that perhaps made sense in those circumstances. Now we can come into our real power and stay there more of the time — if we're shown how.

The Field is an equal-opportunity provider. It doesn't matter if you are a stay-at-home parent, a CEO, or someone who serves customers across a counter or across the world every day. It's up to you to make the choices that will optimize your life. In the Field everything is possible. Yes, you *can* meet your family's needs and your own as well. You just have to approach life differently. The time is ripe for a new way that will allow us to take personal power and accountability to higher levels.

> Every person and every thing is operating in a single energy field, and we each have much more power to create our lives than we ever imagined.

WHY CHANGE?

Lynne McTaggart, an award-winning investigative journalist, reports that many prominent leading-edge scientists still agree with Einstein about his unified field theory. On the most fundamental level, the human mind and body are not distinct and separate from their environment but are bundles of pulsating energy that constantly interact with this vast energy field. "These subatomic particles have no meaning in isolation but only in relationship with everything else," reports McTaggart.[2]

In other words, we're all connected. The very atoms that make up everything are interdependent, always interacting with one another. The events of 9/11 and global natural disasters in recent years have made this connection tangible. Worldwide differences fell away when nearly everyone on the planet felt linked in their shock and grief.

Though in the Field this connection is always at work, it often takes great stress or loss or catastrophic events to remind us of how interdependent we all are. In the Field we are energetically connected — to each other, to the results of our choices, and to our futures. The very next choice you make directly affects what will happen to you next. Even if you don't relate to physics, you can probably relate to this: you have far more power than you ever thought possible because you are part of what's happening, not just an observer of it. Instead of working harder to achieve your goals, you can choose to consciously tap this energy field and create what you want.

This is what people commonly refer to as being "in the zone," that space where you break through into synchronicity and everything clicks. Doors open. Obstacles melt away. Golden opportunities materialize. But on those other days, when nothing works, you can't seem to do anything right, and you descend into what feels like the Black Hole, you're also playing the Field. You're just making choices that amplify that reality.

So, you may be asking, why can't we operate "in the zone" at will? Well, we can. And I can show you how. We need to remember that the Field is always there, whether or not we pay attention to it. It reminds me of the year I left for a trip to Australia on September 7 and arrived on September 9. My birthday happens to fall on September 8. Technically, September 8 didn't happen for me. Did I turn a year older? Of course. And to presume otherwise would be a bit ridiculous, because time did pass. It's the same thing with the Field. It is always there, whether or not you recognize it. If you choose to stay conscious and play the Field, you can change your life in the very next moment.

Twentieth-century technology focused on mundane forms of energy, even as twentieth-century scientists (like Einstein and others) grappled with the Field. In communications, for example, we have evolved from rotary telephones to satellites, to wireless Internet connections. This is nothing compared to the power of the Field. In the twenty-first century we are groping for a usable Field technology, and movies like the 2004 *What the Bleep Do We Know!?* are beginning to bring these ideas into popular culture. Galileo knew that the sun, and not the earth, was the center of our solar system before the rest of the world accepted this truth. Columbus knew the world was round. The Egyptians and Greeks had proven both these facts more than a millennium before, but most people of Galileo's and Columbus's times denied these fundamental truths of nature.

The Field is another fundamental truth of nature, but it's not yet visible or measurable. You've no doubt experienced this connection in the Field that transcends time and space. You think about someone in another state, and minutes later they call, or you know something is wrong with your child before he says a word. Homes and businesses have energy too. You can feel it the moment you walk in the door. You also feel energy in music. As the research on the Mozart Effect has proven, our brain functions differently depending on the music we hear. In Japan Dr. Masaru Emoto has demonstrated that water changes its crystalline form when researchers change their thoughts or expose the water to various types of music or photographs.[3] The implications of this interconnectedness are stunning, and we don't need to understand all the scientific studies to experience it and reap its benefits. It's a lot like the Internet. I can send an email from the middle of the United Arab Emirates on my wireless handheld Blackberry, and a friend in Chicago receives it within minutes. We don't have to know exactly how this works to enjoy the advantages of this new tool.

In some ways, women are particularly equipped to take this leap. Like the quantum field, women have always been dynamic, their moods and chemistry fluctuating with lunar cycles, sensitive to even slight changes in their environments. Many women are in tune with what's happening right now. Their default state is connectedness, and they don't naturally tend to use force to create outcomes. The Field validates what women have always known on some level: that the softer, "feminine" yin skills have as much, or more, power as the charging-ahead yang ways. Women know the Field's energy and connection. The way they respond to various environments, or to another person, is an energetic experience. In fact, most women have experienced the Field in the form of intuition, but they've been unaware that it's always available to them.

In the Field everything is created, including all the possibilities that stretch before you right now. When I refer to the "energy" of the Field, I do not mean whether you feel tired or refreshed in the morning or if you have the stamina to get through your day or if you feel strong enough to take the stairs instead of the elevator at work. Energy refers to this invisible connection. Have you ever seen a zoom-in from a satellite that first focuses on the earth, then your continent, then your state, then your city, then your neighborhood, all the way to your house? Tapping into the bigger energy of the Field is like the reverse: instead of focusing on our one little reality, we expand dramatically into multiple realities and possibilities, most of which allow us to live larger, more fulfilling lives.

Everyone has had these experiences. Most of us just don't know how to live like this daily. The potential of the Field is the elephant in the room that no one is talking about in everyday language. Energy is present in every transaction and interaction. It's in the email you just wrote. It's in the article you just read. It's also in the laundry you didn't fold and in the checkbook you didn't have time to balance. It's in how you feel about the dirty dishes in your sink. It's in your intention for the staff meeting or family vacation. It's in the review you just gave. It's in the thought you just had about your significant other. It's in everything you say or do.

GETTING A HIGH RETURN ON ENERGY

If you can set aside the old belief that we are each trudging through life alone and instead tap into the powerful energy that's all around you, you will be able to transcend circumstances that normally would pull you down. We all have access to the Field. How you choose to tap into it is up to you. Even when you feel depleted and think you have no choice, you always do.

Today businesses and individuals want to leverage their resources and create the most value — in money, business, client retention, and life. In business meetings you'll often hear the term "return on investment," or "ROI," discussed. Businesses have limited resources but want to receive the most in return for those resources, and they plan ahead, research, and find the best possible strategies for making their resources pay back dividends. This same principle can be applied to energy. If you're investing significant energy in a situation, make sure it's commensurate with your yield. In other words, make sure you get a high ROE, or return on energy. In business and in life, you sometimes may not feel as if you have a choice about how and where you invest your energy, but you do. You make crucial decisions every day. If you're going to spin your wheels and not get anywhere, realize that your high- or low-energy choices are creating that spin. The more familiar you become with the range of high- and low-ROE choices, the easier it will be for you to see when you're living an accountable and powerful life. For example, if you know that arguing with your spouse always gives you a low ROE, you may ask yourself why you're investing your energy this way and stop, mid-sentence.

You are the only person who controls how you respond to the situations life throws at you, and you can always decide to make high-ROE choices. Low-ROE choices deplete your resources and originality and create more drama in your life. High-ROE choices enable you to become more effective. Energy doesn't vanish. It just changes form. You choose the form, based in power (high ROE) or fear (low ROE). You just forget sometimes because you are stressed out and act before remembering that you can connect into something bigger than your next action.

THE OLD WAY OF DOING: FORCE

If you're like most people, you often try to control and overpower things, using your energy to force and manipulate individuals and situations. Instead, if you choose to stay conscious and play the Field, you can make an impact on your life immediately. This may feel confounding and disorienting at first because the way the Field works is the opposite of cause and effect. Instead of doing something to cause a result, you clearly state your intention — and the result finds *you*. Your challenge is to *let* it find you. Intention is the key to accessing the power of the Field. Rather than working harder or muscling an outcome, focus on what you want. Zero in on the *what*, not the *how*. Most of us spend our lives trying to make things happen, which sends the message to the Field that things must be made to happen. When you know you can instead operate from power, much less effort and work are entailed. For example, if you are going to a party and want to make contact with a specific person, you can try to force it by planning every little detail of what you will wear, say, and do, or you can set the intention of having a powerful connection with that person and then just go to the party. Think of all the time and energy you will free up when you stop trying to control and engineer what happens.

Think of the Field as a cosmic version of QVC, the popular home-shopping channel. They both have everything you could possibly want, are "on" twenty-four hours a day, and are waiting to fill your order. With QVC, you see what you want. With the cosmic QVC, you imagine what you want, and you don't have to figure out whether to shop online or by phone or determine the size, model number, or which credit card to use. You just need to be clear about what you want to create in your life.

My friend Jessica knows how to "place an order." She wanted to get married and have a child. She was very specific about these intentions. She didn't worry about the *how*. The years went by, her biological clock was ticking, and still she hadn't met the right man, so she decided to adopt. Most people expect to get married and then have a child. Jessica didn't get stuck worrying about the sequence. You've probably guessed the rest of the story. She met her husband, a single father, months later at a school event she would not have attended if she hadn't been a parent. People who have mastered this way of being, who can move into the Field and stay there most of the time, are the ones we call lucky. Most of us just don't believe we have the power to be "lucky" too.

David R. Hawkins, a psychiatrist and director of the Institute for Advanced Theoretical Research, provides some guidelines for operating in this new world. He found a way to measure the levels of energy involved in various choices and to calibrate how operating at these different levels influences the way we live as individuals, families, groups, and countries. Hawkins's extensive research has linked various energy levels to emotional states, attitudes, perceptions, mental processes, worldviews, and spiritual beliefs to create a Map of Consciousness that delineates and quantifies the various levels of personal growth. His fundamental belief is that "force can bring satisfaction, but only power brings joy. Victory over others brings us satisfaction, but victory over *ourselves* brings us joy."[4]

Whatever we focus on creates a field of dominance, according to Hawkins. In his book he recounts how he discovered hidden energy patterns he calls attractors: "Attractor energy patterns have harmonics, as do musical tones. The higher the harmonic's frequency, the higher the power."[5] Think of your "frequency" as the level you operate from and the signal you send out. It's a set point, a homing device, your personal sonar that sends out a signal and attracts people and experiences with similar frequencies. The higher the frequency, the easier your access to high-energy choices, people, and situations. The lower the frequency, the easier your access to low-energy choices, people, and situations. Hawkins underscores the power of intention in the Field: "A sincere desire for change allows one to seek higher attractor energy patterns in their various expressions."[6] For me, this means that every morning when we wake up, whether we realize it or not, we connect to an energy pattern that creates our day. In this book I will explain the power of operating at high or low frequencies and what each can bring to our life.

Most of us have directed our energy toward controlling and manipulating other people and situations instead of using it to tap into the Field. We have used it for force, not power. Though you may want to, you can't make people do something they don't want to do. And in business especially we get seduced by force. Here is an example of how easy it is to fall into that state of mind.

During my fifteen years in the employment industry I worked with Patrick, who ran the most profitable region in the United States. He was one of the most gifted salespeople I'd ever met, and he was also one of the weakest administrators. Every other month I would fly to Texas to spend time with him, and on each visit I would remind him that I needed his weekly reports. As long as I hounded him about not getting his paperwork in on time, neither of us got what we wanted.

When I redirected my energy I realized that what I really wanted was for him to be even more successful. What had I been thinking? Here was our top salesperson, and I had been giving him grief about paperwork! I redirected my energy from force to power. We finally agreed that he could turn his reports in every other month and that they'd be prepared by one of my employees in the regional office in Chicago. Think of all the energy wasted traveling to Texas to hassle him about admin policy when I could have been asking him how I could best help him do his job better!

When you send an intention out into the Field, you place an order with the cosmic QVC. When you opt for force, you set a tone that often gets played out to your disadvantage. For example, if at dinner with your family you dominate the conversation with your concerns about an upcoming vacation, a nice meal can become a family battle, ending with cries of "I didn't want to go anyway!" from the kids. If you create a "force field" at work, people become more focused on who messed up rather than on how to fix or learn from the mistake. Hidden agendas surface that conflict with overall objectives. This also shows up as funky communication with family and friends. Instead of a spirit of cooperation and partnership, each person views the other as an obstacle or, even worse, as an adversary.

You know that force is being used when a conversation with your best friend, who always seems to understand you, suddenly derails and you both leave feeling "off." Other symptoms of force include micromanaging, suspicion, and negativity, which I'll describe later in more detail. Clearly, these things feel bad and don't work too well. Knowing this, why don't we always opt for more powerful behaviors? Because force is familiar, and we forget we always have a choice.

THE NEW WAY OF BEING: POWER

Life is not about controlling and forcing things. It's about power, the power to choose how to use your energy. When you're operating in that paradigm of control over others, you experience a low ROE, because it's impossible to control others or their reactions. You may get temporary spurts of high ROE, but ultimately, you'll always land with a low ROE because you can't control outcomes. When you operate from a place of power, controlling only yourself and your actions, you'll always have a high ROE, because you're staying awake and making good choices. You can control those choices. That's all you can control. When you're in that place of power, you are fully, consciously connected to the Field and will reap its benefits that much faster.

When you try to control, you get entrenched in right and wrong, do's and don'ts, and ego-based thinking, engaging on a lower-energy level and creating a false sense of power. Your real power lies in your ability to use your energy to connect with other people and the potential that brings. This isn't the same as force. According to Hawkins, "Power gives life and energy. Force takes these away."[7] I always felt justified in hounding Patrick for his reports, and it didn't feel good to either of us. When you make high-energy choices, you are able to move through the heaviness and burden of a situation and access wisdom, no matter how difficult the circumstances. You are able to cope with challenges and get back in balance quickly. At work, meetings end on time, you reach consensus, and there is a flow of positive feelings. At home, there's more harmony. Making high-energy choices creates an atmosphere of trust and well-being that's contagious and spreads to your personal relationships as well as to your work teams. There's no space for vengeance or retaliation, making it easier to deal with tough issues. Picture yourself as the eye of the hurricane: you have all sorts of outside pressures frantically whirling around, yet you remain calm. You can begin right now to tap your real power.

PLAYING THE FIELD

In what parts of your life are you using force?
In what parts of your life are you using power?

Playing the Field is not something we master. It is a way of life. I've been playing the Field for most of my life. That doesn't mean the challenges go away. I'm always working on this, and I always will be. Once, on a trip, I met a wonderful man whom I thought was "the one." The connection between us was extraordinary — unlike anything I'd ever experienced. He was in a long-term relationship that was winding down and indicated he was interested in me as well. He gave me just enough hope to stay connected with him. Two years later, he had not ended the other relationship. When we were together, everyone could see the connection between us. I was eager to begin the relationship, but when I tried to be charming, or to influence him, or when I thought about why we should be dating, or why his girlfriend wasn't right for him, I lost my connection with my power because I was attempting to control outcomes.

Because I was making the relationship all about him and what *he* should do, I felt miserable. It got to a point where the thought of not knowing if we were moving forward held up every other aspect of my life. Suddenly, all decisions and activities were connected to this one question: Will we be together? *I'd love to ask him to join me on this vacation, but I'm not going to do it if we're not going to be together, so maybe I'll delay the vacation until I know they've broken up.* This kind of thinking created a ripple in the Field that completely disempowered me because suddenly all my energy was focused on trying to control the *how* instead of ordering the *what*. The more time I spent engineering it, the lower ROE I got.

I revamped. First, I sent out the intention, *Hey if he's the right guy, bring him on; if he's not, bring the right one.* To reconnect with the Field, I remembered the intention I set before we ever met: *to be in relationship with a man whose heart is open and available and to be loved to the depths of my heart, body, mind, soul.* Instead of fixating on trying to help him become that person, I focused on my intention. By operating in the new way, I've been able to move on toward what I want. Now I recognize very quickly when I am operating in force and no longer spend time attempting to force a relationship based on potential. I am also having far more fun. I have freed up a huge amount of energy and am now able to enter into relationships wholeheartedly.

PLAYING THE FIELD

Can you think of a time when your choices in a relationship (personal or professional) were based on force, not power?

M-FIELDS

Playing the Field means operating at higher levels. These can look like flashes of genius, brilliant inspirations, or a new perspective that instantly transforms a situation. Biochemist Rupert Sheldrake has coined the term *morphogenetic fields* (M-Fields) to describe the invisible organizing patterns that act like energy templates. When runner Roger Bannister broke the four-minute mile, he created a new M-Field. When the Wright brothers flew, they created a new M-Field.

Sheldrake contends that it's possible to create increasingly larger and more powerful M-Fields. When Hillary Clinton became the only former First Lady in history to run for Congress, she created a new M-Field. When Oprah Winfrey became the first black female billionaire, she created a new M-Field. Whenever people live a bigger possibility, a new M-Field is born. After that, the possibility for others to do the same increases. If you can learn to play the Field, not only do you make quantum leaps yourself, but you also make it easier for others to take those leaps as well.

PLAYING THE FIELD

Have you ever experienced others creating a new M-Field?
Have you ever created an M-Field for yourself?

THE TEN ENERGETIC CHOICES

The Field offers us a view of life from a place we're not used to being in because it asks us to change the way we approach everything. The greatest challenge in playing the Field for most people is that it's difficult to apply these hard-to-quantify concepts to everyday life. When you've got to pack the kids' lunches and be out the door in five minutes, how do you stop and contemplate the connectedness of everything?

I learned to tap the Field and developed some of these principles as a result of suffering from severe, life-threatening asthma as a child. The upside of asthma was that it made me into a warrior. I came in fighting, and I fought it all the way. After surviving those first five years, I knew I could do anything. Because I could read my body better than the doctors could, I learned to rely on myself and believed it was up to me to make things happen. For the next twenty years, I set out to conquer my various worlds: school, sports, career.

At school, kids called me Windbag because I breathed funny. I fought that with humor and with the determination to show them I could do anything. In third grade I became the first girl patrol captain. I was the first female class president of my high school class. I became the first person in my family to graduate from college and to earn a graduate degree. I lived by slogans like "No pain, no gain" and "Where there's a will, there's a way." Whatever I set out to do, I achieved.

Always on the fast track, proving I could beat the odds, I took an entry-level position at a large global corporation after college and became their youngest vice president ten years later. By thirty-six, I was running a $100 million operation. The harder I tried and achieved what I wanted, the more force and will I applied.

My early patterns of setting up goals, relentlessly pursuing them, and forcing them through served me very well, and to this day I am grateful for the asthma because it gave me so much. But along the way, some of those choices that became my blueprint for life stopped working.

It was a gradual process. The act of succeeding against all odds had become a comfort zone for me, and I unknowingly re-created these situations over and over so I could play in a game where I'd mastered the rules. I knew how to be the underdog. What I didn't know was that staying in a comfort zone led to other choices that kept me from the life I wanted to create. I looped through the same pattern over and over — only faster — and created huge drama. The more force I applied, the more often I brought about the things I most dreaded. When additional force didn't work, I head tripped, wondering what I could do differently, and then repeated the pattern again.

I finally noticed that the choices we make in our response styles to the ups and downs of life have either high or low energy. Over time, I refined these into ten distinct behaviors, or energetic choices, and gave them names. These ten choices, which I list below, are specific, easy to follow, and don't require a degree in physics or philosophy to grasp:

1. COMFORT ZONES: Just because something feels familiar does not mean it's the most powerful use of your energy, and it can lead you even lower to:

2. HEAD TRIPS: Mentally replaying the same scenario and what-ifs over and over wears you down and leads you to make an even lower-energy choice:

3. LOOPS: Repeating the same patterns and drama from situation to situation, job to job, and relationship to relationship becomes an unconscious template for your life that leads to the lowest-energy choice of all:

4. MAGNETS: Your negative, fear-based beliefs can actually create what you are most trying to avoid. You are so depleted, this lowest-energy choice sucks you into the Black Hole.

5. SUSPEND JUDGMENT: Letting go of your interpretations of and opinions about others, outcomes, and especially yourself will immediately take you out of the Fear Zone of low-energy choices and expand your possibilities.

6. LIGHTEN UP: Lightening Up (especially on yourself) shifts the intensity and opens a new way of operating that catapults you into the Power Zone.

7. TUNE IN: It's time to unplug from the wired world and get present with the human being in front of you right now. When you connect with someone else, the result is more than twice as powerful than if you don't.

8. SCAN: When you Scan, you move into a detached state of observation, using all your senses to take in the physical, emotional, and intuitive information in your environment. More knowledge gives you more options.

9. TAP THE TRUTH: You tap your greatest power when you live in integrity with yourself and with everyone else.

10. BELIEVE: What you deeply, authentically Believe, you create. And the power you experience expands your potential. This highest-energy choice propels you into Breakthrough.

Which of these choices do you make?

Remember, you access the Field by deciding to. By choosing. You choose your intention, and then you choose your next action. Playing the Field is about the hundreds of energetic choices you make every day and what these choices create. I will show you how to make better decisions, create less stress and drama, find greater meaning, and enjoy a more accountable life — in good times and in bad. We will explore each of these choices in depth throughout this book. The next chapter introduces the Energy Spectrum and provides a big picture of the ten energetic choices. Chapters 3 through 6 describe the low-energy choices, and chapters 7 through 12 the high-energy ones. Each chapter contains questions to provoke further exploration as well as summaries of all the ideas discussed.

At the beginning of this chapter, I told you about Timothy, our Guardian Angel who appeared to drop in from nowhere. Let me close with a story of how to use these choices in more mundane situations.

ORDINARY DAYS IN THE FIELD

My friend Jill is a widow and a mom who spends much of her day behind the wheel taking her children to school, sports events, and various lessons. One afternoon she found herself in the unusual position of being all alone in her van with the prospect of one whole discretionary hour. Traffic was heavy, and a potential traffic jam might limit how much time she actually had. Could she make it to the grocery store and back in time to pick up her children? Get that overdue oil change? Have the car washed, so the fast-food leftovers in the backseat didn't start growing mold? She decided to relax and enjoy the sunny day instead of grousing about the delay or the wasted opportunity.

Suddenly Jill noticed the new Trader Joe's. One of her closest friends was having a big birthday in two days and was obsessed with a particular wine that only Trader Joe's carries. Jill hadn't had the time, or the inclination, to even figure out where the store was, let alone to deal with the traffic, so she'd completely given up on the idea of getting the wine for her friend. Yet because she chose to enjoy the sunny day, she was later able to delight her friend with that special birthday gift.

Each choice affects your future. This time you might notice Trader Joe's. Next time you find a good babysitter out of the blue. After that, a job offer comes to you before you even realize you're ready for a change.

Jill could have chosen to stay in a foul mood because of the traffic and missed Trader Joe's. Later, she might have dismissed a flash of genius about a challenge she was having with one of her kids because everything felt too overwhelming to her. She then could have met Mr. Right at the gym, only to brush him off because she felt as negative about herself as she did about everything else. Use your energy consciously. When you're moving fast and making decisions on the run, know that each choice counts. These examples may seem inconsequential, but that's the whole point: though the everyday choices you make can seem quite small, over time you will get better and better at playing the Field, and the results will become bigger and bigger. And what could be more exciting than an ever-expanding life?

SUMMARY

- Everything is energy. We all have a supply. How you choose to connect to it is up to you. Even when you feel depleted and think you have no choice, you always do.

- We spend much of our energy trying to change and control people and things (force).

- Playing the Field, a new way of living and working, is a view of life from a place we're not used to being in (power). Because this new way is nonlinear, we can do away with the labor involved in cause-and-effect and if-then thinking.

- The Field encompasses everything, and in the Field anything is possible.

- Everything you say or do causes a ripple in the Field, and other people pick up on it, even though it's very subtle. A shift occurs, then sets off a chain reaction.

- The ten powerful choices available to us determine whether we are using our energy toward a high or low return.

- By understanding all the ways you're using your energy, you can choose a more efficient and more satisfying way to act when you're feeling unproductive, frustrated, and hopeless. You will evaluate situations more quickly and make an impact, regardless of your personal or professional situation.

CHAPTER TWO

THE ENERGY SPECTRUM

Have you ever had one of those days when you felt invincible? When everything clicked and went your way? And then there are those days when nothing works. Why does it seem as if the perfect days are so few and far between? Why is it so much easier for a day to go from bad to worse than from good to great? In this chapter I will explain how this happens and what you can do to create more good days. Below is a story about one of the bad days, and later I'll tell you how I turned it around.

One Monday morning I was rushing to leave on time for work, but my house was on the market and it had to be picture-perfect before I left. I was concerned that my cats might mess up something, and, on cue, my younger cat deposited a hair ball on the white carpeting. Scrubbing it out delayed my departure. I left a note for the contractor who was coming over to finish some work, saying that I would be available by phone only between 10:00 a.m. and 1:15 p.m. if he had any questions.

I hadn't packed for the gym the night before and pulled everything together in a rush. In the shower after a less-than-satisfying workout (someone was using my favorite stair stepper), I realized I'd forgotten to bring my earrings and belt. At the El, my transit card didn't work. I kept ramming my right hip into the turnstile until the attendant drawled, "Lady, go get a new card." I walked all the way back to the entrance to get a new card and missed my train. Then I realized my lunch was still sitting on the kitchen counter.

At work, I was frantically preparing for a speech I had to give in Washington, D.C., the next day. I'd intended to finish my PowerPoint presentation earlier in the week but had gotten sidetracked. Josh, my right-hand man, was deadlocked in a dispute with two other members of my team. Susan, our client, was beginning to pick up on the fact that something was wrong. She had already left me two voice mails and an urgent email.

I would have called her back immediately, but I was on the phone with one of my clients in London finalizing the details of our annual contract, needed, of course, that day. I rushed the discussion with him to a close just in time to make a conference call about our upcoming conference in Iceland.

As this second call dragged on, I went into my email to respond to Susan, drafting one of my most eloquent replies ever. Just as I was about to hit SEND, my computer crashed.

I silently cursed as I realized this work of art had forever vanished. *Why does this always happen when I'm about to go out of town? This is going to put me way behind, and we might even lose Susan as a client.* I noticed how bad my nails looked and thought, *Oh, well, a manicure is not going to happen today.* I mentally drifted off, thinking of what I needed to do before my flight the next morning: 1) Pick up my clothes from the dry cleaner. 2) Get a prescription from the drugstore. 3) Drop my car off at the dealership. 4) Slap on another coat of nail polish.

It was only 10:00 a.m. *How did I let things get so out of control? This happens every time I go out of town. I get absolutely crazy. I know I must be contributing to this, but how? What am I doing to create this?*

In the past I might have blamed my boss for my workload, the economy for my slow-selling house, or my lack of a husband for the chaos at home. But I am no longer fooling myself. I know I am responsible for the life I create. I had created the day's chaos, and I could create calm. I had just forgotten to play the Field. Your life can change in an instant. In the Field, each of your choices either makes problems bigger, plunging you into the Black Hole, or catapults you into Breakthrough — a space of high energy and possibility.

> In the Field you can choose the Black Hole, or you can choose Breakthrough.

WHY CHANGE?

Perhaps like you, as a child I was instilled with a belief that if I worked really hard and did everything I was supposed to do, I would achieve my goals. I followed the Newtonian cause-and-effect thinking that if I did A, then B would follow. When it didn't, I thought it was my fault. I didn't fully understand that life works differently. It's an interactive dialogue that involves all six of our senses, not a one-sided monologue that doesn't allow for possibility and listening. No matter how much effort you exert, obstacles will always land in your path — that's just the way it is. That's the moment to take responsibility instead of feeling hopeless and without choice. Your power is directly connected to your next choice.

Think about the biggest issue you're dealing with right now at home or at work. How much of your energy (or your significant other's) is this consuming? If this problem were solved, what would that free you up to do as a family or couple? What if you had the skill to also deal effectively with the next challenge and the one after that? (Because they will keep coming.)

Once you experience this way of living, you won't want to go back to the old way. This is not about eliminating the "bad" things in life. It's about embracing all aspects of yourself so you understand when you're making high-energy choices and when you're making low-energy ones. If you can live all these realities at once, you will understand how each choice can move you out of the Fear Zone of low-energy choices and frustration and into the Power Zone of high-energy choices and possibility, and you will be better able to navigate in the Field. It's not about changing the parts of you that always make low-energy choices. Rather, it's about accepting the spectrum of experiences that are available to you, and as a result, being catapulted to another place on the Energy Spectrum (which we'll discuss in more detail in the next chapter). This process is not even conscious. You'll see the impact of each choice you make and how some choices open doors and some don't. To put it simply, you have far more power than you realize.

THE OLD WAY OF DOING: THE BLACK HOLE

We have all come of age in linear, hierarchical systems, whether in families, school, the workplace, or volunteer organizations. Many of these situations make us feel powerless. Everyday events like renewing our driver's license or getting through to the cable company to schedule an installation can feel frustrating and discouraging and can spawn a contagious side effect: complaining. It's hard not to feel like a victim. That very mind-set, however, makes us vulnerable to more of the same.

In space, a black hole is a strong gravitational entity that devours everything coming in contact with it. I use the term to describe those times when you feel as if you have no control and descend into frustration, anger, depression, or hopelessness. All these are low-energy feelings, and the Black Hole flourishes on them. Negative thinking can also lead to the Black Hole. A black hole is created from a star that's collapsed, and the gravity is so great that no light escapes. "Darkness" and "collapse" also describe how you fall into the Black Hole in life.

Darkness results from the monotonous demands of day-to-day living like washing the dishes, getting groceries, and taking the kids to soccer practice. It can also come from misunderstandings and miscommunications. Your Internet service provider goes down. You argue with your neighbors or friends. Bills or important papers get misplaced. This kind of drudgery can erode your energy. You refer to this as having a bad day or a bad week. It can be crazy making and often features a cast of thousands: the car-pool mom who's always late picking up your child, the clerk who can't ring up your order, the employee who doesn't show up on a critical day.

When you've *collapsed* in the Black Hole, the issues are more profound and can catapult you very quickly into a deep, deep place. *Collapse* can come from a trauma like a death in the family or a daunting diagnosis. You're laid off. You discover your child is using drugs. You experience a midlife crisis and wonder if you want to stay married. This aspect of the Black Hole usually involves your values and purpose in life and causes you to question who you are. You are typically struggling with life-and-death issues that make you wonder about the very meaning of it all:

What's the point anyway?
I can't get through this.
This is more than I can bear.
How will I go on?

You usually grapple with *collapse* alone, even if you're with a partner or family member. You become more inward and introspective, often redefining who you are in the world. People can offer comfort, but this is not about escaping the pain.

Ironically, you feel much more agitated in darkness, while in collapse, you're beyond agitation. You're in a profound state of grief and metamorphosis. And you can experience both aspects of the Black Hole at once. With a death or divorce, you are reeling from the profound pain of separation, even as you have to deal with all the bureaucratic and social requirements like making funeral arrangements, finding attorneys, doing paperwork, moving, and beginning a new life.

During his mother's funeral, Jamal, a medical equipment salesperson, received two messages on his cell phone. One came during the service, and one as they were lowering his mom into her grave. They were both from his boss in California asking why Jamal hadn't turned in his sales numbers for the month. The following Monday morning, Jamal told his boss, "I think you were very insensitive about my mother's death."

A month later, Jamal's boss took away more than half of his sales territory (and income), including a pending $2 million sale. Jamal knew it was time to move on. Over several weeks, he worked through both aspects of the Black Hole at the same time. In collapse, he grieved the loss of his mother and dealt with the challenge and shock of needing to find a new career. In darkness, he planned his exit, reviewed his finances, and helped to wrap up his mother's affairs.

It's much easier to descend into the Black Hole than it is to ascend into Breakthrough. Low-energy emotions and limiting beliefs are more tempting than positive emotions. They take less effort because we are familiar with them. Even though we prefer high-energy feelings, we gravitate toward low-energy ones because they're comfortable. We don't have to be accountable and change our behavior or solve the problem. We can just complain and blame. And misery does love company. You'll find lots of people who'll back you up and add some complaints of their own. Remember Hawkins's attractor pattern: like draws like. Your choice to complain is a free pass to low energy and away from being responsible.

But these low-energy emotions and the victim mentality pull you away from the life you want. The second you doubt or diminish yourself, you step into the Black Hole. The more you feed it with worry, fear, anger, stress, and other energy-depleting emotions, the larger it becomes and the faster you sink, making it harder to get out.

If you watch *Star Trek* reruns, you may recall one episode in which the more lasers Captain Kirk shoots into some dangerous amorphous blob, the bigger it gets. Similarly, the more hate, negativity, and judgment you throw at a problem, the bigger it gets. Life looks harder. Everything feels more challenging because your internal expression has gone from a can-do, open approach to a dark place of scarcity that affects your family, your job, and everything you touch.

When you feel threatened, it's natural to hide until conditions are safe again. But pulling away removes you from the opportunity right in front of you to interact with the situation and move through it. Your answer is in the very feeling or person or place you're trying to avoid, and this will keep recurring until you deal with it. It won't go away. It will just come up in different forms, and more intensely.

I call situations and events that instantaneously plunge you into the Black Hole "triggers." Everyone has different triggers, involving relationships, self-esteem, money, or success. They can begin with something as seemingly minor as feeling slighted by a friend or wondering about accounting practices at work. Even companies can have triggers. During the past several years newspapers have chronicled the stories of major corporate, financial, and religious institutions falling into the Black Hole because people did what their bosses told them, thought they were untouchable, or they figured that the end justifies the means.

One of my Black Hole triggers throughout my life has been my sisters. We have never been very close. Since I was chronically ill throughout much of my childhood, understandably my sisters came to resent all the attention Mom and Dad gave me. For years I romanticized the idea of having sisters and thought we should be best friends. But they weren't actively in my life, and I wasn't involved in theirs. We all protected our turf with Mom and Dad, and as adults this translated into frustrating vacations in Washington, where everyone lived in a different part of the state. Instead of simply recharging with my folks on Whidbey Island, I would spend the entire week crisscrossing the state because no one could agree on a time when we could all get together. This process always resulted in drama, hurt feelings, and tears. Finally, I redirected my energy and acknowledged the relationship for what it was instead of the romanticized notion I longed for. Then I realized that the pain of interacting in these low-energy ways had become greater than the pain of changing. I decided I didn't need anything from my sisters and risked disappointing my mom and dad, who had wanted us to be close. Ironically, I actually began to enjoy my sisters on a deeper level.

Unless you learn how to make high-energy choices, the Black Hole will leave you feeling depleted, discouraged, despairing, and even less able to find your way out. Until now, many of us have lived according to three fundamental beliefs that promote this kind of limited, low-energy way of life. Let's take a look at them now.

THE TRIPLE THREAT

I call these three beliefs, which are actually delusions that set us up to avoid accountability, the Triple Threat. How many of these ideas have kept you from playing the Field?

1. You have control.

So much of life is all about process, hierarchy, structure, and control. You try to control your children, other people's opinions of you, or how your spouse dresses. Sometimes you actually believe you can control everyone and everything. But you can't. Here is an example of how some parents' need for control overpowered their shared goal of providing a quality experience for their children. Everyone involved was operating from the low-energy choices of the Energy Spectrum, and the focus was on who was in charge rather than on the children.

One Saturday morning at 8:00 my friend Elise, a psychologist, arrived at the renowned children's theater two hours early to ensure that her son could register. The spots in these classes were in great demand. Elise was the first parent to arrive, and it was unclear where and how the registration would be handled. As other parents showed up, she set up a simple "take a number" system so that people could come back when registration officially opened and be served in order.

When she returned just before 10:00, she could tell that something was wrong. The air was charged. Staff members were scurrying back and forth. People were confused. The director strode out, furious. "Who is responsible for this?" she roared, holding up the numbering system.

"Well, I am," Elise replied meekly.

"I have never seen anything so stupid! Who are you to change the system I have been using for so many years? I can't believe you did this. How are you going to fix this?"

One dad, an engineer, spoke up: "But I think this is obvious. We should continue the numbering system."

A parent shouted from the back of the room, "But then people who came in late wouldn't get help," not realizing the outcome would have been the same without the numbering system. Chaos ensued. The fight for control divided the crowd. This well-educated group of adults began to act like children. A Stanford professor demanded that her son be signed up, and a company president shouted her down. The director turned purple with rage. Her need for control outweighed her need to serve the parents or their children better, causing her to miss the opportunity right in front of her to make a high-energy choice to resolve the situation. This is the power of your choices on the Energy Spectrum. You can move quickly in one direction or the other.

Many of us try to take control at work as well. Heather, one of my former colleagues, ran a successful sales operation while being very much a rebel and taking huge risks. During one budget cycle we were falling short of our income goal, so she arbitrarily decided to impose a midyear rate increase. We discussed this at the executive meeting and asked her how our clients would respond.

"I brought in the account. They've known me for ten years. They won't question this," Heather replied. "I'll make it small enough that they won't notice it on a weekly basis." She then implemented her plan aggressively. Margins increased, profits went up, and Heather was headed for an incredible bonus.

At the end of the year, however, when the clients recon-
ciled their account, they discovered the increase and became
furious. They not only demanded a refund, they fired us!
Heather scrambled and got them back, but only after conced-
ing even bigger discounts than before. The relationship was
severely damaged, negatively affecting business results. The
first two quarters of the following year were particularly
rough as the client learned to trust her again and slowly built
back the business. Low-energy choices, like being less than
honest with a client — or anyone for that matter — always
come back to bite you.

2. You can't be yourself.

Many of us are like chameleons: it feels completely normal
to act different ways in different settings. Are you the same person on the inside as you are on the outside? Are you the same
with your children, your spouse, your friends, and your co-
workers? Playing a role suppresses the parts of you that most
want expression, and this exacts a toll on your creativity and
emotional well-being. Because of this underlying frustration,
you are less patient and more likely to take things out on others.
As a result, you may descend into inappropriate behavior at
work or at home, shifting you into lower-energy choices. Everyone has experienced a well-intentioned email that went south
suddenly when the author forgot to edit his thoughts before hit-
ting SEND. It's much easier to pound out those words when
you're not face-to-face with people. When you have to deal with
the fallout later, you're already headed for the Black Hole.

On the flip side, my friend Denise, COO for a multimillion-
dollar company, has to stay on schedule and be very driven to

accomplish what she needs to every day. When she gets home, sometimes she forgets to turn it off and continues issuing orders. Her husband helps recalibrate things by saying, "Honey, I'm not one of your direct reports." He reminds her that it's okay to be who she really is and to step out of her COO role when she's at home. It works every time.

3. You come last.

Many women invest in their futures and in their families' futures, with the idea that they must put in their time now so that they can have the life they want later. This might mean pursuing money and success and spending less time with their children as they're growing up, waiting until they're fully vested in their 401(k) before making a job change, or waiting until the kids are out of the house before exploring their dreams.

If you put yourself last, you'll be treated as last. Remember, the Field takes its cue from *you*. Put yourself first. Care for the caretaker. Choosing to serve is different from being a martyr. If you stay home with your children out of fear or a feeling of obligation, you're operating from force, not power, because you're trying to make something work that doesn't inherently support your best interests. Instead of saying, "I'm not going back to work right now because my family needs me at home," say, "I'm not going back to work right now because I choose to be home for my children."

When you put yourself last, you voluntarily spend more time in the Black Hole, and you become a victim. Fortunately, these old beliefs (you have control, you can't be yourself, and you come last) no longer apply.

THE NEW WAY OF BEING: BREAKTHROUGH

In the Field you can choose the Black Hole, or your can choose Breakthrough. Who wouldn't choose Breakthrough, if they could? With the Black Hole, the problem is knowing how to get out. With Breakthrough, it's knowing how to get in. The greatest challenge for most people is making this shift from Black Hole to Breakthrough every day.

This is a different way to operate. I am inviting you to embrace a broader view of life; I'm asking you to live big. Don't assume that the Black Hole is bad and that Breakthrough is good. They just "are," and sometimes you need the Black Hole to reach a higher level of Breakthrough. The gift of the Black Hole is that it can highlight needed changes and motivate you to act. When you're in the Black Hole, particularly in *collapse*, you can move from rupture to rapture if you're willing to stay open and learn. You are always one choice away from creating a different outcome and experience.

PLAYING THE FIELD

Describe situations in which you have lived each of these Triple Threat beliefs:
You have control.
You can't be yourself.
You come last.

You can fall into the Black Hole instantly. You can also instantly experience your next Breakthrough. It's all about choice. The four low-energy choices (Comfort Zones, Head Trips, Loops, and Magnets) spring from your need for control, taking you off center and needlessly consuming your resources. In contrast, the Power Zone choices (Lighten Up, Suspend Judgment, Tune In, Scan, Tap the Truth, and Believe) give you a high return on your energy.

In the Black Hole, we shut down, lose access to greater possibilities, and feel as if there's no way out. In Breakthrough we collapse time and move instantaneously to what we want. These ten choices leverage time and space in all parts of life and help you take responsibility for what you're creating, no matter what's in front of you.

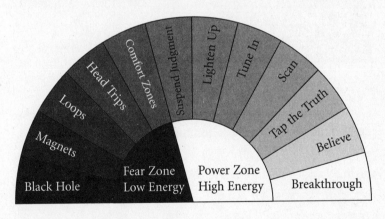

In the Fear Zone, one choice cascades into another, gaining momentum and sucking you into the Black Hole. In the Power Zone, any of the six choices can create Breakthrough. It's also possible to "mulitzone." Within seconds, a woman might find herself Suspending Judgment about her teen's messy room, while getting caught in a Head Trip about an upcoming dinner party and Tapping the Truth to create greater closeness with her spouse.

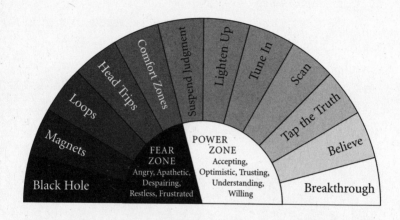

In the Fear Zone, you feel emotions such as restlessness, anger, frustration, despair, and apathy. If, on the other hand, you're feeling willingness, acceptance, understanding, optimism, trust, or engagement, you are in the Power Zone. This model helps you to instantly see how you are using your energy.

THE POWER OF GOING TO NEUTRAL

You have an array of choices on the Energy Spectrum. As you move away from neutral in either direction, you accelerate, descending into force and the Black Hole, or ascending into power and Breakthrough. Your response to a situation will largely dictate what happens next. If you make a high-energy choice, you will tap into more power and possibility. If you meet low-energy behavior with a high-energy response (an upset Head Tripping employee approaches you, and you Tune In and listen before responding), you'll get a different outcome than if you meet them at their level. Typically, when you get caught in a low-energy choice, you don't realize it until you're out of it and can see things more clearly.

The point on the Spectrum between Comfort Zones and Suspend Judgment is a portal to Black Hole or Breakthrough. You can create what's in front of you by fully accepting all the realities inside you. These can be voices from places in you that hold pain and fear. And they can be the voices that carry hope. But the Field can't do its magic until you go to neutral and let the emotional charge of a situation dissipate. That doesn't happen until you realize what parts of you have been triggered. And remember, if those aspects of you are based in the Fear Zone, those realities will probably feel frightening or unnerving. The Power Zone voices will feel uplifting and inspiring. That day at the children's theater, everyone was so entrenched in the Fear Zone that they lost the ability to navigate the Spectrum and focus on what mattered most — registering the children for class. When you can accept these multiple realities, you can quiet all the voices and move to a different state of being.

You may feel as if I'm asking you to learn a whole new way of living when you're already overloaded with everything on your to-do list. While I *am* raising the bar in one sense, I'm lowering it in another. You just have to take small, consistent steps, which I'll spell out for you with lots of examples. In the next moment, making breakfast for your family, driving to work, or perfecting downward dog in yoga class, you can make high-energy choices. The combined effects of the high-energy choices you make each day will be profound. You will live your way back into your power, creating the life you want.

By understanding all the ways you're using your energy, you can choose a more efficient and more satisfying way to work when you're feeling unproductive, frustrated, and hopeless. You will evaluate situations more quickly and make an impact, regardless of your personal situation or the position you hold in your company. As you learn to opt for high-energy choices, you'll feel not only less stressed but more fulfilled at the end of every day.

THE ENERGY EDGE

With each choice, over time, your life will expand exponentially. I call this the Energy Edge. It's important to understand that the impact of your choices, no matter how insignificant they may seem, is cumulative. With each high-energy choice, it becomes easier to make another, and you get bigger results. And when you make high-energy choices, you are often greeted with an assist, a sign that you are going in the right direction. With my sisters, once I made a high-energy choice, they responded to me at that level, and the old conflicts began to fall away. On my next visit, they both offered to come to me, instead of making me drive to their homes.

The Field is cumulative in one other important way: the greater the critical mass, the more amplified the results. The more people playing in the Power Zone, the more of a boost we all will experience. It's also true that the more people there are making low-energy choices, the greater the power of fear in the Field and in the world. As more and more of us make high-energy choices, the expression "a rising tide raises all boats" will be clearly at work. Can you imagine being surrounded by people who take responsibility for their lives and live in Breakthrough?

The Field amplifies everything. It's like compound interest or basic financial planning. You can be like some of my friends who played big and invested everything in the stock market, lost their retirement savings, concluded investing doesn't work, and walked away, or you can start small and methodically, work at it over time, and realize a big return. For example, if you begin saving $1,000 a year starting at age forty-five and it earns an average of 8 percent, you'll have $48,913 at age sixty-five. If, on the other hand, you begin when you're twenty-five, your total at age sixty-five will be a whopping $267,653. The sooner you invest in high-energy choices, the greater the ultimate return will be.

If you remember how to calculate the area of a square, you get the idea of the magnitude of small changes (see diagram on next page). If the side of a square is one inch, the area is one square inch (1 x 1). If we double the length of the side, the area quadruples (2 x 2 = 4). If we triple the length of the side, the area become nine times as great (3 x 3 = 9). Little changes create

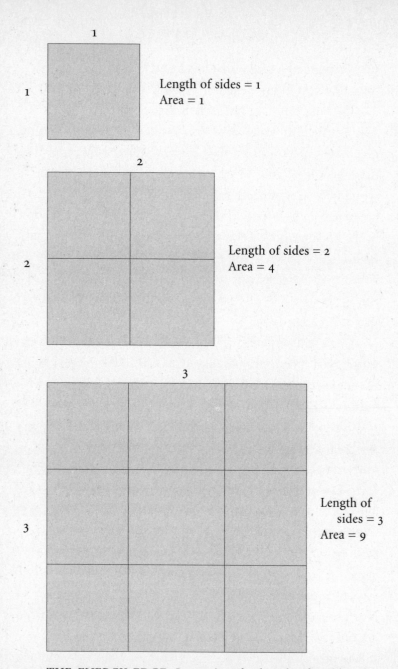

THE ENERGY EDGE. Increasing the length of a side of a square increases its area exponentially. So, too, small changes in our choices can have exponential effects on our lives.

big results. Here's a story of a little change I made one night that eventually created huge results in my professional life.

When I was thirty-one, my career was kicking into high gear. To my amazement and delight, John Bowmer, the brand-new CEO, invited me to dine with the executive team and him at a posh restaurant. I wore my most attractive suit, my best jewelry, and my favorite shoes. I had gone over all the financials for my area of responsibility in case he had any questions. But despite all these preparations, I felt extremely uncomfortable. The whole power meal experience was new to me, and I didn't know how to make small talk with people at that level. And there I was, seated right next to Mr. Bowmer, who was very British, very powerful, and seemingly very proper!

The room was stiff with formality. Its dark mahogany wood and deep red carpets and drapes were accompanied by classical music and more knives, forks, and spoons than I had ever seen on one table. The sommelier and maître d' addressed us in hushed tones, and waiters scurried around, pulling out our chairs and whisking the napkins onto our laps, like toreadors.

I'd picked up one of the most perfect sourdough rolls I'd ever seen, then realized I had no idea which bread plate was mine. I froze. I couldn't very well put it back. I looked around the elegantly set table in vain for a clue. Swallowing hard, I set it on the small plate to my right and hoped for the best. The senior execs made small talk, dancing on the edges, unsure of how best to please Mr. Bowmer. I worried about my bread. After a few minutes, Mr. Bowmer turned to me with a twinkle in his eye and quietly said, "Are you enjoying my bread?" As if we were in a movie, all talk stopped. Everyone at the table zeroed in on me to see what would happen next.

All my insecurities lined up, beckoning me into a low-energy response on the fear-based end of the Energy Spectrum. *Brenda, you are so out of your league. His watch probably cost more than your car. One false step could blow your career.* But I knew I had a choice, so I searched for a high-energy response. I asked myself, If I'd been born on the "right side of the tracks" or weren't so insecure, how would I react?

I took a breath.

"Well, *you* weren't eating it!" I joked, flashing him a big smile.

And he laughed. Actually, he howled.

Everyone exhaled, and the conversations resumed as the atmosphere lightened up. I had chosen the power end of the Energy Spectrum: courage, not fear. Instead of getting horribly embarrassed and apologizing, I spoke from my power. Had I let the fear take over, I would have fumbled, apologized, tuned out for the rest of the meal, and missed out on loads of opportunity.

One of my friends has used the Energy Edge powerfully in the area of relationships. Susan had been happily married for twelve years and had two children. Before she met her husband she had had a messy breakup with Tom, a man she knew from college. They had dated seriously for five years, and the relationship had ended in frustration and anger, with some important things left unsaid. Every few months her mind wandered to Tom, and she wondered what he was doing and if he was happy. Their twenty-fifth college reunion was approaching, and Susan signed up for it nine months in advance with the intention of seeing Tom and having some sort of closure to their relationship, even though his name wasn't on the roster of those attending. As she flew from

Washington to Wisconsin for the event, she put out the intention: *just create a space for connection*. In other words, she placed an order with the cosmic QVC and paid no attention to the how. She simply focused on the what.

The reunion went from 3:00 until 11:00, and fifteen hundred people attended. When Susan entered the building, the first person she saw was Tom. With an eight-hour event in a hall with so many people and multiple doors, what were the chances that they would have connected so quickly? Susan had let the Field do the work for her.

When you're operating in the Power Zone, conventional time lines don't exist, and your ability to create is only bound by your imagination. You can manifest what you want in an instant. The Field moves quickly when everything is in sync. Susan had sent her intention out into the Field and easily found the closure she longed for. Though they did not discuss the details of the breakup, they were kind to each other and supportive of the way one another's lives had turned out. Although Tom wanted to be friends with Susan and invited her to meet his wife and children, she felt satisfied with their conversation and didn't feel the need to begin a new friendship. It was clear that time had romanticized their relationship and that what had happened had been the right thing all along. What you're seeking is seeking you. Use the Energy Edge.

FROM BLACK HOLE TO BREAKTHROUGH

You may be wondering how the crazy day I described at the start of this chapter turned out. So let's pick up where we left off. My voice mail was full, and the phone kept ringing. I knew there were a couple of emergencies among the messages. I could tell I was headed for one of those days when I just couldn't keep up. *How am I going to handle all this? I'm two hours into my day, and it's already insane. Will I have time to back up my presentation? Can I get to the dry cleaner so I can wear my lucky suit? If I don't get the car into the dealership before I go, the warranty will expire. When can I take it in? I have to get this done today. What if it breaks down and it's not under warranty?*

I knew I could stop the descent into the Black Hole by making high-energy choices that would immediately pop me back into the Field.

First, I called a halt to all the clamor and mentally went to neutral. That cleared my mind, giving me more direct access to the Field. Second, I realized that I had to stop the Head Trips. I quieted the mental jabber, then reviewed the challenges I was facing so I could make some deliberate choices. The pharmacy was on my way to the El, so I could pick up my prescription on the way home. I called to confirm that they were open late. I took a breath and realized I had to let go of the graphics in my presentation. Also, nothing was actually wrong with my car. It was just the last free tune-up before the warranty expired. With the next breath, I decided not to deal with the car at all. With a quieter mind, I was able to finish the London contract, because I was fully focused on it, and I wasn't leaking energy worrying about all the other fires I had to put out.

A half hour later my computer crashed, but miraculously I didn't lose my presentation. Out of the blue, the VP of marketing stopped by. He made my presentation look five times more professional in just minutes. I did what I needed to do at work, took care of my errands, and got to the airport on time. My presentation was a big success. The following week, I called the auto dealer. It was two months past warranty, and yet he knew I took care of my car. He extended the warranty, because each time I'd been there, I'd made the high-energy choice to get to know him instead of just doing paperwork in the waiting room.

Unhappy starts to stressful days can be turned around when you play the Field.

SUMMARY

- "Good days" and "bad days" result from our choices.

- Take responsibility. Life ebbs and flows. You create the quality of your life with your choices, and your power comes from learning how to navigate the ebb and the flow, not in eliminating, ignoring, or steamrolling through the tough times.

- Four low-energy choices (Comfort Zones, Head Trips, Loops, and Magnets) move us into the Fear Zone toward the Black Hole.

- Go to neutral to stop the negative momentum and make higher-energy choices.

- Five high-energy choices (Suspend Judgment, Lighten Up, Tune In, Scan, Tap the Truth, and Believe) move us into the Power Zone and toward Breakthrough.

- Get familiar with the Energy Spectrum. As you move away from neutral in either direction, you accelerate, descending into fear and force and the Black Hole, or ascending into courage, power, and Breakthrough.

- Don't let the Triple Threat hold you back. Watch out for these limiting beliefs:

  - You have control.

  - You can't be yourself.

  - You come last.

- With each higher-energy choice you make, over time, your life will expand exponentially. The Energy Edge will become your winning edge. This process is cumulative, and the more often you make these choices, the more powerfully and quickly you're able to create increasingly powerful results and Breakthrough.

PART TWO

THE FEAR ZONE AND ITS FOUR LOW-ENERGY CHOICES

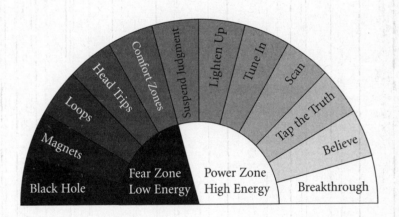

CHAPTER THREE

COMFORT ZONES

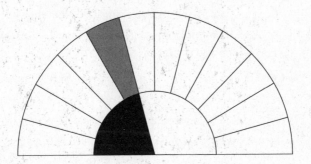

Have you ever sincerely wanted to change something in your life, but no matter what you did, you kept running into the same obstacles or self-defeating patterns? That's because lifelong Comfort Zones live powerfully and deeply in our subconscious. Surface change will not be effective until we bring these out into the light. Here's a story about one of my Comfort Zones that may help you deal with yours.

Uncle Art sped toward the hospital as I leaned forward, clinging to the dashboard and trying to breathe. My lips were turning blue, and he was breaking the speed limit, hoping to attract a police escort so we could get there faster. I vomited all over the front seat as I passed in and out of consciousness. For the first time I thought I might not make it.

I had begged and insisted that my parents let me try camping. I so wanted to be a normal kid. Driving to Blue Lake with Uncle Art and my three cousins had been one of the happiest times of my life. Just after I crawled into my sleeping bag, the wheezing started. I tried to control it, willing it to go away. But it didn't. I fought it all night, and in the early morning I woke Art and said I needed to go to the hospital. I could barely breathe.

It took more than an hour to get to the nearest hospital. The nurses and orderlies were yelling questions at him, but Art didn't know anything. I'm sure he was scared to death.

"The shot! The shot! The shot!" Frantically pointing to my arm, I tried to force the words out of my throat. They strapped down my feet and arms. When they started to force me back, I would fight with all my might because that position made it even more difficult to breathe. "Brenda, stay with me," the orderly said.

The nurse scrambled in with a syringe of adrenaline. I saw the needle and smiled inside. As the drug entered my system I felt warm and tingly all over. All was well. I would soon be able to breathe. When I came to, Art looked sick. The orderly held my hand until my dad got there, and when he walked in I felt safe. High on adrenaline but very weak, I sat up and asked, "When do I get to go back to Blue Lake?" When you cannot do something as basic as breathing, it puts everything else into perspective. No drama in life or in business can ever equal that experience.

The ability to stay calm under extreme duress served me well as I went after school leadership positions and sports achievements. In my career I've been known as someone who can face the most challenging situations with a cool head and restore order. I became an extremely effective mediator because I could detach from positions and focus on the perceptions and communications of the people involved. The more volatile the scenario, the better I did.

I would look for insurmountable odds in my work challenges because they seemed so insignificant compared to what I had survived in my early life. I became really good at reading anxiety levels in people and intuiting what they were thinking. And because I knew how to step away from the fear and to leave myself, becoming a detached observer, it was easy for me to walk into new offices, new regions, and new positions and make an impact fast. It didn't occur to me to feel afraid.

COMFORT ZONES

Just because something feels familiar
does not mean it's the most powerful use of your energy.

Seeking challenges has been a significant lifelong Comfort Zone for me, and I also have many smaller Comfort Zones, like keeping my desk and my home orderly and starting my day with a perfectly brewed cup of coffee. To recognize your Comfort Zones, start identifying the small ones, and the bigger ones will emerge. Do you always order the Caesar salad at lunch? Pick the same type of friends? Read the same sections of the paper each day, starting with sports? Have you had the same haircut for the last decade? A Comfort Zone is the place you go to because you know how to be in it. Your Comfort Zones are a life blueprint that you follow unconsciously. Without realizing it, you make choices that keep you in the familiar. And even though the familiar may not be the healthiest place to be, it's where you know how to behave. Often your friends and family and co-workers will recognize it before you do because they're not as emotionally invested. Until you become conscious of this process, you'll always pick the known over the unknown.

A Comfort Zone is neither good nor bad. You just need to notice when it has stopped serving you. And at some point (often at midlife) your Comfort Zones stop working and become obstacles to your fulfillment and happiness. In fact, they lead to longer and longer periods in the Black Hole. The more emotion you have over giving it up, the more anchored your Comfort Zone becomes to past events and the less likely it is to be connected to what's happening now. To tap the full power of the Field, you must redefine your Comfort Zones.

A Comfort Zone can be a state of mind, like being a victim or staying angry at the world. It can be a behavior as small as trying to make those around you laugh and feel comfortable, or it can be a tendency not to deal with conflict. Your lifetime blueprint can show up in the person (or people) you marry, the way you interact with your children, the role you play at your job, or the inability to see your own beauty because you're a size sixteen. Do you have friends who always play the class clown or who always date people who aren't available? Nine times out of ten, we go on autopilot and gravitate toward what we know, even if ultimately it makes us unhappy.

WHY CHANGE?

When you go to a Comfort Zone you initially feel some immediate relief. You have learned the landscape well. You know how to navigate the rugged terrain, the plateaus and the shortcuts. Though you may not even particularly like this territory, you have mastered how to move through it.

Though some Comfort Zones are innocuous, they all mask some need. With less healthy Comfort Zones, after the initial relief of familiarity, your emotions kick in, letting you know that, though you appear to be moving forward, you're really not. You feel like something is missing. You know you're in a Comfort Zone because no matter what variation you try, whether you walk fast or take a shortcut, you're still there. It can be crazy making.

Many of us love working under pressure and feel it keeps us focused. But have you ever made a snap judgment that you regretted? Or completed a project of lower quality than you had wanted because you ran out of time or energy? Maybe you don't even like working under pressure. If you try to change, though, chances are that your mind and body are so programmed to function this way that they will override you. You'll delay and procrastinate and manage to re-create the pressure you crave.

Emotionally you may want out. Every fiber of your being may want out. But you can't seem to *get* out. If you feel stuck, if you've lost your passion, or the fire in your belly, chances are you're in a Comfort Zone. If you're very busy and engaged but still feel dull and uninspired, you're in a Comfort Zone. If you're going through the motions and keeping up but lacking in enthusiasm and excitement, you're in a Comfort Zone. Even if you feel as if you're trying to change, that won't happen until you really recognize your Comfort Zones and begin moving out of them.

You don't always know you're in a Comfort Zone until things start unraveling. They start unraveling because the way you've been operating isn't serving your highest purpose. When you break free from a Comfort Zone, you create opportunities for huge movement in your life. Like a snake shedding an old skin, you are ready to grow. The old form has served you well, but now it's time to live larger. In the words of Anaïs Nin, "And the day came when the risk it took to remain tight inside the bud was more painful than the risk it took to blossom."[1]

With my level of comfort in chaos, I constantly sought more challenge, more money, more promotions. The bigger the challenge, the bigger the rush. Each time I achieved some impossible task, they raised the bar, and if they didn't, I did. I wanted that hit of adrenaline I'd learned to crave.

One day this stopped working. I woke up and realized that I was so focused on staying in my Comfort Zone that I didn't even know if I was happy with my life or my work. I did know, however, that I'd lost all my passion.

If you don't break out of a Comfort Zone, it can become a Loop that eventually grows into a Magnet (discussed in chapters 5 and 6). When you break free into new territory, you become engaged and interested in life on a different level. Your passion returns, and you may reinvent yourself and redefine who you are in connection to your family, friends, your work, clients, and co-workers. You invite in new people, new ideas, and new situations you hadn't imagined or allowed for while operating in the familiar. But achieving this new rapture sometimes requires a rupture from your lifetime blueprint.

THE OLD WAY OF DOING

Most people settle into routines. They make a plan for their lives and move forward in lockstep, without ever evaluating it unless they experience some major disruption like a death or disaster or midlife crisis. Sometimes when you operate in a Comfort Zone it begins to feel unreal, more like the Twilight Zone. You created many of your Comfort Zones in early childhood as a way to feel safe. We may go through many Comfort Zones in our lifetimes, only letting go of them when the pain becomes great enough.

The old way is more dramatic. The old way creates victims. You always have the opportunity to expand your life, but until you realize this, you will continue to live out assumptions like:

- Life is hard.

- No pain, no gain.

- If I don't put in the time, I won't reap the rewards.

- I can enjoy life when I retire.

Security and control will drive most of your decisions. And the familiar does provide a sense of control. I'm not saying life isn't difficult at times, and not to do your best, but when you're getting the signals that it isn't working, it's time to move out of your Comfort Zones.

THE NEW WAY OF BEING

As we've discussed, Comfort Zones can be tricky to identify. At some point it will occur to you that what has worked until now is no longer serving you. Sometimes you change bit by bit, and sometimes a big event transforms you on the spot. You may have to be in a Loop a few times before you step away completely from a Comfort Zone. In my case, I set increasingly larger goals, managing higher and higher levels of adrenaline. After a ski accident blew out my knee, I spent two weeks in bed and was then in an immobilizer from my right hip to my ankle for three months. I came to a full stop for the first time in my life.

I regrouped. As a result, I was able to recognize and move out of my lifetime blueprint of chaos. You won't need a major life change to get your attention if you follow these steps:

1. When things aren't working, notice what's familiar.

Are you trying everything, and still nothing's going right? Identify what's the same. That's where the question and the answer lie. Many of us gravitate toward the same kind of partner or spouse, and even though we pick different people, the situation always seems to end up the same. You may have a female friend who always has tyrannical bosses. Or you may know a man whose girlfriends always leave him for someone else. You've watched these wonderful people over the years date people who seem different on the surface but who are really the same old thing. They're not aware that they keep revisiting these Comfort Zones.

As in the opening story, it's often significant childhood events that define the Comfort Zone. Why do these women select men who don't commit, and why do these men keep picking unfaithful women, even though that's not what they want? They want to be in a committed relationship. They honestly do. But by gravitating to the familiar, they fail to get what they want.

You've no doubt noticed a similar phenomenon in your life. Don't judge yourself. Your Comfort Zone behaviors usually sprang from a need to survive and have served you well in the past. Although I am enormously grateful for the asthma in my early life, it also added a Comfort Zone that brought a high level of intensity into much of my life, and I felt bored when I didn't have it. When I began to construct my relationships and my jobs to re-create this level of intensity, it wasn't healthy and didn't serve me.

PLAYING THE FIELD

What do you notice not working in your life?

What is familiar about this?

Which Comfort Zones do you recognize in your relationships, your family, and at work?

Which Comfort Zones no longer serve you?

If you can't see the Comfort Zones that no longer serve you, which friend, relative, or advisor might be able to help?

2. Zero in on the real issue.

Often you may not even realize that your Comfort Zones, like a favorite pair of old tennis shoes, are not giving you the support you need. When you're in a Comfort Zone, you've got a blind spot and often don't perceive the Zone until you're ready to break free. Find the blind spot. A friend, therapist, teacher, mentor, or boss can point it out, if you will let them.

Another way to zero in is to ask yourself, "If I were to remove all the fear from this situation, what would I want? In a perfect world, in which I'm not worried about status or finances, what would I do ?" You can get to what's important when you cut away the extraneous. You can't receive from someone what you don't give yourself. If your child is numbing out with drugs and alcohol, ask yourself how you are numbing out. If you're bent out of shape because your boss won't empower you, empower yourself. If you keep gravitating toward noncommittal partners, perhaps you are not committed in some way as well.

I have selected men who aren't emotionally available. It was easier and safer for me to be the one who worked for the relationship and overextended myself because this was familiar. I knew how not to be on the receiving end. When my best friend, Laurie, asked me why I was attracted to these sorts, I instantly realized it was because that's how my early relationship with my dad was. It was on his terms, since he worked two jobs to pay my medical bills. And when I used all my energy to manage the chaos I'd created by having a relationship with an emotionally unavailable man, I couldn't be available either.

PLAYING THE FIELD

Choose one Comfort Zone that's not working.
How is this pattern familiar?
What does it remind you of? Did you do something
*   similar as a child?*
Do you see any sort of lifelong pattern?

3. Take the next step.

Once you detach from a Comfort Zone, both you and it begin to change. When you notice a Comfort Zone you can begin to move toward high-energy choices, but it will take action to get you all the way there. Picture how you want your new life to be. What steps will you need to take to move you toward this new way?

I was once on a board of directors for a community organization with a woman named Jenna, who drove everyone insane. She always wore an incredibly disagreeable expression, argued frequently, and loved to debate. She was extraordinarily active at lobbying and would bring up issues outside board meetings so she could rally support. She was both devious and divisive.

The good news about a mind like hers is that we need this type of thinking to shake things up. Critical thinkers help the greater good become even better, but Jenna took this too far. I knew that at the heart of this situation was a Comfort Zone. When we sat down to talk about it, I asked her why she operated this way. She told me she was quite unhappy and very insecure and that she goes to the other extreme to compensate. She hadn't realized the extent of the negative impact she was having on our board and began trying to move out of this behavior.

At the next board meeting, she succeeded. Instead of coming off hard and argumentative, she arrived at a brilliant solution to a problem we were having by focusing on it a different way. The rest of us were floored. We were used to her squashing everyone else's ideas but not offering a solution. Everyone was so surprised at the positive change she had made. At the following meeting, however, Jenna went back into her Comfort Zone. That's what we do, we move in and out of it. Sometimes you take a step forward, and sometimes you take a step back. The important thing is to catch yourself whenever you can.

PLAYING THE FIELD

What one step can you take to break free of your Comfort Zone?
How will this restore your passion and enhance your life?

4. Hang in there.

Your decision to change a lifelong program is significant. You will feel friction before letting go. This new way of being won't feel familiar, and you may find yourself doing things to get back to the familiar, lower-energy Comfort Zone. Psychologists Gay and Kathlyn Hendricks call this an "upper limits" problem and the core to every challenge we face.[2] When things get too good, we find a way to reduce our good feelings back down to the familiar. The greater the struggle, the more deeply rooted we become in the Comfort Zone.

Keep in mind also that other people get used to your Comfort Zones, so when you begin making changes it will take a while before people respond to you at this new level. Some people won't trust that you've really changed, and others may prefer that you stay in your Comfort Zone because it meshes perfectly with theirs. For example, Jenna's talent for chaos created an opportunity for me to be the voice of reason and for others on the board either to pull back or to complain that no one appreciated their ideas.

When you move out of a Comfort Zone it challenges everyone in your life to move out of theirs, either because of your inspiring example or because your Comfort Zones are interdependent and you have disrupted the interaction. Whole family systems have transformed because one member changed; some family members may not like it. But don't let others' discomfort hold you back.

PLAYING THE FIELD

How will moving out of this Comfort Zone affect others?

Who might be threatened by your desire to leave your Comfort Zone?

What is being served by your return to this Comfort Zone?

What would it take to move on from this Comfort Zone?

How can you hang in there?

DAN'S NEW PROGRAM

Because I know how difficult it can be to move out of a Comfort Zone, I want to share an inspiring story that demonstrates how dramatic the results can be when you do. When you leave the familiar behind, anything can happen. Dan was a friend of a friend of mine who felt like he was carrying a huge load. He had a pretty good life — a great life, in fact, by most people's standards — but he wasn't happy.

Dan attributed his Comfort Zone to his Irish heritage of trudging forward through a hard life. His particular version of this legacy felt like the hard work and heavy burden of parenthood. Dan had worked in a number of companies in technical positions and had a comfortable salary, but it didn't feel like enough, with four children to put through college. He'd tried to catch the Silicon Valley brass ring by starting a successful company of his own, but after three attempts that swallowed up huge amounts of time, money, and energy, nothing had panned out.

Dan wanted to be a good parent, and he also wanted to be happy. He loved technology, and there were some new developments he wanted to devote some time to, if only he didn't have the burden of a full-time job. One day in 1985, taking a walk and mulling over this dilemma, he had an epiphany: his kids were all smart. If they truly wanted to go to college, they'd find a way. He didn't really have to finance all four of their educations. His wife made a good living, and even if she weren't working, he calculated that they could live on just $19,000 a year if they trimmed expenses.

He discussed this idea with his wife that night and told her that what he really wanted to do was to get involved with this new technology called the Internet. Dan felt that there were great commercial possibilities, but there were no guarantees, and there would be no steady paycheck, at least at first.

With his wife's support, Dan informed his kids of his shift in thinking about their educational futures and began talking with colleagues about his ideas for the future of the Internet. A few months later, he organized a new conference he called Interop to bring industry leaders together to discuss business and the Internet. They began meeting annually in San Jose, and a few years later outgrew the convention center there and moved to Las Vegas. Dan was famous for roller-skating through the exhibits and knowing everyone. By 1990 the conference had grown to two hundred exhibitors (some of whom later became the first Internet-based companies) and twenty thousand attendees. Ziff-Davis Publishing purchased the show that year for a whopping $25 million.

Dan continued to follow his passion, ultimately founding nine other companies, including one of the first Internet shopping-cart services. He ultimately earned more than $100 million and earned the nickname "Mother of the Internet." Dan's decision to break free from his Comfort Zone is the reason you and I have access to the Internet today.

SUMMARY

- Just because something feels familiar does not mean it's the most powerful use of your energy.

- Your Comfort Zones are a life blueprint that you follow unconsciously.

- A Comfort Zone is not good or bad. You just need to recognize when it has stopped serving you.

- And at some point (often at midlife) your Comfort Zones stop working and become obstacles to your fulfillment and happiness. In fact, they lead to longer and longer periods in the Black Hole.

- The great challenge of a Comfort Zone is that it feels so natural and familiar that it's difficult to recognize when you are in one. Often your friends, family, and co-workers will recognize it before you do because they're not as emotionally invested.

- When you break free from a Comfort Zone, you create opportunities for huge movement in your life.

- When things aren't working, notice what's familiar.

- Zero in on the real issue.

- Take the next step.

- Hang in there.

- When you move out of a Comfort Zone, you challenge everyone in your life to move out of theirs.

CHAPTER FOUR

HEAD TRIPS

Have you ever repeatedly relived a situation in your head, making it much worse than it really was? When you Head Trip, in anticipation of all the what-ifs, you expend a lot of energy. You bounce from the past to the future, spending little time in the present. You make a what-if more real than what has actually occurred. While Comfort Zones are often unconscious, Head Trips are *very* conscious. In fact, you create them. Here is an example of one of the biggest Head Trips I ever experienced. My traveling companion was my mom.

We were both very worried about my dad. He had recovered

from a quintuple bypass years earlier but was again having heart trouble. The doctors did not want to try another bypass, and the situation did not look good. Since my father was twelve years older than my mom, we had always assumed that my mom would become a widow, but this was still very hard to face. So what did we do? We planned. We planned how we would handle that scenario. We were proactive and talked about everything from the financial impact to where mom would live. We did everything we could to brace ourselves for something that terrified us. We didn't include Dad in these conversations. We wanted to spare him and help him maintain a positive attitude.

We did this for seven years, spending many of our holiday visits and vacations talking about these eventualities instead of just living and being in the moment. Based on our justified but ultimately untrue assumptions about Dad's demise, Mom also made several choices about her lifestyle. She dropped out of the community band, where she played clarinet, and gave up touring with the church choir. She spent all her free time with Dad, and even though I tried to talk her into coming to Europe with me a couple of times, she didn't want to leave him behind.

More than ten years later, Dad is still going strong. He is the oldest of thirteen children and one of four who are still living. My friends still refer to that seven-year period as "Dad's deathwatch."

Although I was glad to be clear about Mom's wishes and to be prepared when Dad does pass, I realize now that all the Head Tripping was a choice my mother and I made that ultimately had no impact on the outcome. Instead of enjoying life and one another, Mom and I invested a huge amount of time, talk, and tribulation on a decidedly low-energy choice.

HEAD TRIPS

Mentally replaying the same scenario and what-ifs over and over wears you down and leads you to make an even lower-energy choice.

Head Trips create anticipatory fatigue about something that will probably never happen. The more energy you expend on this type of mental exhaustion, the more it grows. The parade of what-ifs becomes more real and more difficult to shut down, and then you get swept up in that reality, taking yourself away from what's happening right now. This causes a split in your energy, where you're physically here but mentally a thousand miles away and days or weeks into the future. People pick up on the rift and may even think that your negativity is directed at them; then *they* start Head Tripping. This contagious dynamic will continue until you make the conscious choice to disengage.

WHY CHANGE?

Overanalyzing creates mental dramas, distorts perceptions, and causes you to project your issues onto family, friends, and co-workers. Simply put, Head Trips are just not the best use of your time and energy. And it wastes the energy of others if you insist that they listen to your paranoid delusions. Think of a time when you Head Tripped and drove everyone around you crazy because you wouldn't let it go. Maybe what triggered it was a date that seemed to go badly. Or a disappointing parent-teacher conference. Or a performance review. It might have involved selling your home or worrying about your teenager or older parent. You're obsessed with "If only I'd done this. If only I'd done that." Is it really helping you to run through this scenario one more time?

Fear corrupts. The drama of Head Trips causes chemical reactions in the body, which wears down under the relentless pressure. The inner static spreads from the mental to the physical, wearing down your immune system and expressing itself as headaches and upset stomachs. Do you know someone who always gets sick before a big business trip or who always throws her back out during a high-stress time?

There's a reason for this. Candace B. Pert, author of *Molecules of Emotion: The Science behind Mind-Body Medicine*, writes, "The molecules of our emotions share intimate connections with, and are indeed inseparable from, our physiology. It is the emotions...that link mind and body."[1] When you make low-energy choices, like Head Tripping, your body responds. Barb, a young mother, told her neighbor, "Watch what happens. We're moving Saturday, and Barry always gets the flu when we move." Sure enough, Barry was sniffling and miserably carting furniture to the truck. Do you do something similarly reliable? After a big work push, do you get a cold? Or lose your voice right before big presentations?

When you Head Trip, you check out and take up residence in the Black Hole, where the drama in your mind becomes more real than what's going on in front of you. As a result, you miss things in your environment that might actually influence your dilemma. But you're so caught up in the anticipatory fatigue that, to feel safe, you start preparing scenarios: *if this happens, I'll do this. If that happens, I'll do this.* Usually you've just spun your wheels and wasted your energy. Poet Wendell Berry writes of the "peace of the wild things who do not tax themselves with forethought of grief," a beautiful way of putting what we human beings so often do when we Head Trip.[2]

THE OLD WAY OF DOING

Western culture rewards left-brain thinking (rules, hierarchy, consequences). These external controls make it easy to disregard our inner voice. Most of us find it much easier to work out of fear than out of contentment and self-assured inner guidance. This makes us susceptible to paranoia. The 2000 Y2K scare was a worldwide example of anticipatory fatigue that tapped into the Fear Zone. My friend's brother-in-law went to extremes to equip their house with extra food, water, and supplies, filling her basement with a three-month supply for her family of five. Do you know someone like that?

Look at the Head Tripping that can happen in a room full of people. The dynamic shifts to the lowest common denominator. Your team at work begins to wonder about layoffs. At family gatherings the conversation often involves the predicaments of relatives who aren't present. With friends, we gossip. When you expend energy on a fear-based story and enlist others to do the same, you fan the flame of a Head Trip, and you may create a Magnet (to be discussed in chapter 6).

On the other hand, if you learn to stop Head Tripping before you start, you'll have more energy to deal with the situation before you. You'll also sleep better. Your mind doesn't just shut off when you go to sleep, and if you've filled it with all sorts of dire scenarios, it will feed them back to you at inconvenient times like 3:00 a.m. So the next time a co-worker makes a doom-and-gloom comment, resist the urge to chime in with more Head Tripping comments. Redirect negative conversations about family members, and refuse to be a conduit for gossip with your friends. Low-energy choices feed more energy to the situation, and you get even less energy back.

THE NEW WAY OF BEING

All Head Trips are based on obsession and fear about the worst things that could happen. Conversely, when you're operating from a place of openness and good will, you optimize your power. When you make high-energy choices, your fear level is very low, and your love level very high. I'm not saying you have to walk into the office and tell everyone you love them. But if you act out of love rather than fear, people feel it and are drawn to you.

Here are some specific ways to curtail Head Trips. If you use these steps, you will also be able to recognize when others are Head Tripping, avoid spinning along with them, and help them stop if they wish to.

1. Become aware that you're Head Tripping.

Sometimes you can catch your negative mental dialogue, and sometimes it may take someone else to point out what you're doing. Following a tough breakup (during which she saw her ex every day), my friend Lauren experienced such emotional ups and downs and felt such despair that she couldn't function. A friend of hers wisely suggested that she not try to psyche herself up (*I can do it! Next time I see him I'll...*). All Lauren had to do was observe how she was doing. Each day she would begin her journaling by drawing one of several different symbols. A circle meant harmony and connection — she was feeling powerful and did fine; she didn't spend the whole day Head Tripping and speculating, *if only I'd done this...if I'd met him sooner*. A square designated an okay but not a great day — she felt uncomfortable and made some low-energy choices but kept herself from being sucked down further. A spiral meant Head Trips and stomachaches — she'd completely lost it and spent the day making low-energy choices. In other words, using this approach, she didn't need to have any answers — she just needed to observe herself. This system helped ground her when the whole world seemed to be wobbling beneath her. It also helped her to understand her triggers.

Sometimes it takes a friend to help you see that you're in a Head Trip. Several years ago I was on a business trip in Florida and was having trouble sleeping. I felt stressed because my company had just been bought, and the new owners would be making big changes. Cathy was an ambitious and competitive colleague who had let the new owners know that she wanted to take over my job. Our meeting schedule that week was intense, and sleep was precious. The next day's sessions didn't start until 9:00, and I was looking forward to sleeping in. In fact, at dinner we all talked about how excited we were at the prospect of a couple of extra hours of rest. Imagine my surprise when I was awakened by a call at 6:00 a.m. from Cathy, asking if she could borrow my Windbreaker for her power walk.

Geez! I thought. *Why didn't she ask me last night at dinner? Why is she waking me up for this? I know. She wants me off balance. She's already made it known she's after my job.* I turned the incident into far more than it was, got all upset, and started my day in the Black Hole. When I met Mindy, a colleague and friend, for breakfast, and spelled out the Cathy Conspiracy Theory, Mindy burst out laughing and nearly sprayed me with her orange juice.

"Brenda, are you insane? Have you lost your mind? Listen to yourself! Did it ever occur to you that she was stressed and couldn't sleep and wanted to walk it off? Listen to what you're saying!"

I was in such a diminished state, I had jumped to a paranoid conclusion but didn't know it until I heard someone repeat it back to me. I realized she was right and stopped my Head Trip in its tracks. Interestingly, I forgot my Windbreaker when I packed to return home the next day. It seemed symbolic that I had left it. I learned that I didn't need the Head Trip it represented anymore.

PLAYING THE FIELD

Do you know someone who has Head Trips regularly? What's it like to be around them?

Describe a time when you Head Tripped about something that wasn't even true or didn't eventually happen.

2. Identify your triggers.

When you are caught up in Head Trips, distorting your perceptions and projecting your issues onto other people, catch yourself as quickly as you can. If you take the time to look at your patterns and recognize your triggers, you may be surprised. You will also be better equipped to short-circuit a Head Trip, which may be a symptom of operating in a darker place than you're conscious of.

Say a friend doesn't do what he said he would do. Thinking *My friend didn't come through for me* may degenerate into *None of my friends come through for me* and then descend even further into *No one ever comes through for me. I must not be worth it.* You may have a certain trigger pattern. One of my friends jokes that her temporary financial setbacks always degenerate into scenarios of becoming a bag lady on the streets of Los Angeles. Use any familiar doom-and-gloom images as an alert that you've begun a downward spiral — and stop them.

Here are some common Head Trip triggers. Which ones resonate with you?

- Aging
- Appearance
- Career
- Love
- Money
- Sex
- Success
- Weight

3. Manage the angst.

When you Head Trip, your body kicks in with symptoms of stress. Your breathing becomes shallower and quickens, your pulse rate goes up, your hands get clammy, and you may perspire. You're in the grip of the Black Hole. Even though you may be trying to stop your Head Trip, your physical symptoms are overwhelming you. Some people find it helpful to walk, run, swim, or dance and to move this energy from their heads into their bodies and out.

When I'm in this agitated state, I remind myself that the world is much bigger than me or the situation at hand. I tell myself, *What will be will be. I don't need to control.* I envision myself as a fleck in the universe, part of something big and vast and encompassing and try to remember my place in this scheme. And if that doesn't work, I play the "one-up" game, taking my fears to an extreme and making them so over-the-top that it's laughable. Figure out what works for you before your next Head Trip.

PLAYING THE FIELD

What is the best way to manage your feelings when you feel triggered?
What has helped in the past?

---

4. Get a reality check.

Shine the light of reality on your inner story. Ask yourself, *Do I have my facts right?* We are all moving so fast and doing so much and juggling so many roles, it's hard to keep them all straight. When your mental energy is invested in something that could happen or has happened, you project various scenarios and outcomes instead of dealing with the now, which always has the greatest influence on the ultimate resolution. You leave your power behind when you go off on these mental journeys of despair.

I write about and teach these ideas, but at times Head Tripping levels me too. Sometimes it takes three or four days to get a reality check. Sometimes it takes months. My Head Trips go through various phases, depending on the intensity of the situation and what it triggers in me.

When I Head Trip, I become distracted because my mind is not on the present. It's reviewing different scenarios, causing chain reactions. Some mornings I realize I haven't noticed when I've gotten into my car and driven to the office. One evening I arrived at the parking garage, stepped into the elevator, and could not recall what floor my car was on because I'd been Head Tripping so much that morning. It took me twenty minutes to find my car, making me late for an appointment.

The energy you invest in reality affects your day as well, only in a more positive way. Once I was dealing with high stress because of some possible litigation at work. When I got into the car, all the physical reactions from stress and fear kicked in. Instead of making my commute a Head Trip, I noticed the anxiety and decided to do my best to stay conscious of my driving and what was happening in real time. Halfway to work, I realized this was the first time ever I'd caught all green lights. I shifted my focus to them. I had packed a change of clothes I needed for golfing later in the day and felt pleased I'd remembered to bring them. *Good*, I said to myself. *You are here. You remembered the bag.* Moments later, as I walked to the office, I realized I was bringing the bag with me. I had meant to keep it in the trunk until I got to the golf course. I'd had another disconnect. Although I didn't keep a complete grip on reality, the fact that I was attempting to was really what mattered.

PLAYING THE FIELD

Describe a time when you got a reality check on a Head Trip.

Who are the best people to give you a reality check?

Whom do you trust and listen to?

---

5. Get out of your head and into action.

If you're Head Tripping about a real situation, you probably know the next step you need to take, and your Head Trip is actually about the steps after that. Chances are the next step is a small and doable one. Take it. In the story above, my next step was to get myself to work. It wasn't to deal with the whole litigation situation. You will find that movement in the moment helps relieve some of the stress and stops Head Tripping momentum.

Sometimes the next step is to identify what the real fear is, to acknowledge it, to do what you can, and to let it go. What's the worst thing that could happen? And if that happened, what would be the result? And if that happened, what would be the result? Keep going until you get to the ultimate fear.

My friend Spencer was laid off unexpectedly and felt paralyzed by his Head Tripping until he used this technique. To him the worst thing that could happen would be that he would use up his savings to support himself until he found a job. If that happened, he wouldn't be able to pay his rent. If that happened, he would have to move home with his parents. If that happened, he realized, he could use his home base to take some classes and expand his skills. He let out a big sigh. He knew he had talent and that he would get another job and that even the worst scenario wasn't that bad. This stopped his Head Trips, getting him unstuck and back into job hunting. As you may have guessed, he never did burn through all his savings or lose his apartment or have to move back in with his folks.

PLAYING THE FIELD

What is the one thing you can do to get out of your head and into action the next time you begin to Head Trip?

6. Let it go.

You've no doubt heard the famous Groucho Marx routine in which a patient says, "Doc, it hurts when I do this" and the doctor replies, "Then don't do it." The chaos in your life reaches various levels, and you deal with it depending on the level. Sometimes you are able to simply let go of a situation that doesn't particularly trigger you. Sometimes just identifying that you're on a Head Trip is enough to stop it. One key is to go to neutral by Suspending Judgment (more on this in chapter 7) for five seconds and ask, What is the greater significance of this right now? Does anything come to mind? Even asking this question shifts energy.

Being with your children can put things in perspective right away and help you let go. For some people, it's seeing a movie, taking a walk, being in nature, playing with their dog, having a massage, listening to music, or working out. Spend time doing whatever calms, centers, and grounds you if you find yourself Head Tripping. In the Black Hole you forget that all these things exist. One of my friends actually keeps a file on her computer called "In emergency, break glass," which lists the things that bring her back to center.

Most of us are so goal oriented that we forget that time can collapse and reality can change. When you're working with the quantum field, the old rules don't apply, and you can create results instantly. My friend Mackenzie hired a low-cost computer consultant who was just starting to transfer her files to his laptop for the home business she was launching. The man didn't sound that knowledgeable about computers on the phone but had helped other clients move files successfully. Mackenzie felt concerned when she had to show the consultant how to remove the back panel from her computer, then even more upset when the man hadn't brought enough CDs to do the job.

Furious, Mackenzie drove to Office Depot nearby to purchase more CDs. *This man doesn't know what he's doing. I'm probably going to lose all my files. If he can just get them transferred I can get going with my client project. But what if he can't?*

Mackenzie stewed all the way to Office Depot, then realized she'd forgotten her wallet. As she drove back home, she caught herself and took a deep breath. *What is this guy triggering in me? He's starting out, trying to build a consulting business, and so am I. He must remind me of how incompetent I feel about starting a new venture*. Mackenzie got her wallet, returned to the store, and bought the CDs. She also picked up some file-transfer software she could use herself if the consultant ultimately wasn't successful (he wasn't). Mackenzie noticed how much calmer she was the rest of the day. Even though she had to wait another week to transfer her files because of a technical problem with her new laptop, she saw a way to continue working on the client project because her mind was quiet and relaxed. If she hadn't let go of her Head Trip, she might have created an even more stressful reality.

We don't learn to let go overnight. When I managed to get connected to reality on my way to work that stressful day, I didn't place a judgment on the fact that I was only able to stay present for three traffic signals. I noticed they were green and enjoyed the moment. Such a little thing brought huge relief. When you're in trauma, ask yourself, *Is hashing through this one more time going to tell me anything I don't already know? This is so painful. What do I have to gain by running through every scenario one more time?* Take small steps. When I recently had to wait thirty minutes in the lobby of my doctor's office, I noticed the very first Head Tripping sentence as it marched through my head and replaced it with, *This half hour is the only quiet time I've had all week, and I'm going to enjoy it.* So I did.

PLAYING THE FIELD

Describe a time when you let go and went to neutral instead of Head Tripping.

What is the most effective way for you to go to neutral?

BOGEYING THE BOGEYMAN

Though it may not feel like it at the time, in every charged situation you have the chance to go to neutral. Notice when you have the first strong emotional reaction. Recognize when your breathing changes or stops. You will feel tense, and your throat will feel tight. These physical symptoms are your cue to go to neutral. It's hard, and you may feel as if you don't have a choice about these reactions, but you do. As you apply these ideas, you'll get better and better at recognizing what type of environment brings on Head Trips. Here's an example of how you can change the experience and outcome of a situation by choosing not to Head Trip. When I flew to Phoenix for a meeting recently, I arrived a day early to golf with a couple of colleagues. Madeline, an associate with whom I'd had regular conflict, decided to organize a golf tournament on that day and coordinated it via email and phone but didn't copy me or include me in the tournament. In fact, she scheduled my golfing partners to play in it without me.

When I found out, I sent her an email asking what was going on. She sent back two very angry emails. Instead of replying with a nasty message or obsessing, I picked up the phone and called her.

She wouldn't accept my call.

This was a situation ripe for Head Tripping. *Why was she trying to take control? Why didn't she want me golfing with those colleagues? What was her agenda? What was she lobbying for?*

Instead of continuing down this low-energy road, I left her a kind message. She never called back, but the important thing was that I didn't go into Head Tripping, saving valuable energy.

At the meeting, Madeline approached me right away and said, "Let's clear the air." Because I was in the Power Zone instead of Head Tripping in the Fear Zone, I was able to have a useful conversation with her before starting the day's business. By choosing to Head Trip, I would have blown this event up, I would have involved my colleagues, people would have taken sides, and much drama would have ensued. By consciously choosing not to Head Trip, I spared myself an enormous amount of anguish. I did get to golf, and I had a wonderful time.

SUMMARY

- When you Head Trip you expend a lot of energy bouncing from the past to the future and spend little time in the present.

- Head Tripping creates anticipatory fatigue about something that will probably never happen.

- People pick up your Head Tripping. They may even think your negativity is directed at *them*, causing them to start Head Tripping.

- Overanalyzing creates mental dramas, distorts perceptions, and causes you to project your issues onto family, friends, and co-workers.

- This negativity goes back into you, wearing down your immune system and expressing itself as headaches and upset stomachs.

- If you learn to stop Head Tripping before you start, you'll have more energy to deal with the situation before you.

- Become aware that you're Head Tripping. Sometimes you can catch your negative mental dialogue, and sometimes it may take someone else to point out what you're doing.

- Identify your triggers. You may be operating in a darker place than you're conscious of. Use any familiar doom-and-gloom images as an alert that you've begun a downward spiral — and stop them.

- Manage the angst. Some people find it helpful to walk, run, swim, or dance and to move this energy from their heads and into their bodies and out.

- Get a reality check. Ask yourself, *Do I have my facts right?*

- Get out of your head and into action. You probably know the next step you need to take, and your Head Trip is actually about the steps after that.

CHAPTER FIVE

LOOPS

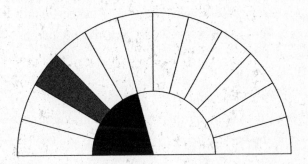

D o you have a dream you've put on hold — that hobby you wanted to pursue or some extra-special vacation? What about that job change you've been contemplating? If you have been attempting to make changes in these areas but have not been successful, chances are you've been operating in a Loop. This chapter will show you how to break out of your Loops so that you can pursue your dreams.

Job changes make you especially prone to Loops because they are loaded with Fear Zone thinking about financial security, ego, and the unknown.

If I leave this job, will I make enough money?
How will I find another?

What if I can't find a better job?
What if I lose my house?

Here is a story about how one woman got out of her career Loop. Eva is one of those people whose left and right brains are amazingly balanced. Since she's so dramatic and theatrical, you would never guess she's a successful IT professional who's sought after for high-paying consulting assignments.

But Eva felt torn. She had always wanted to pursue a career in voice-over, and to that end she saved her money and took time off to develop this career. But it wouldn't take off. She would dip her toe into this other world, and every time the fear that it was never going to work started getting to her, she'd go back to what she knew — IT. Two years would slip by in the blink of an eye. Her dream had still not happened.

Discouraged after eating through her savings yet again, Eva decided to step away from her dream and took an assignment in New York. Two years had passed since she had moved, and during that time Eva had taken a hard look at the choices and patterns in her life. She was exhausted from the seventy-hour workweeks, and though she had paid off her debt and replenished her savings, she had once again put her dream on hold. And then the thought occurred to her, *Why can't I do both?* Her all-or-nothing approach was a Loop that she had been in for several years. She was so tired of the results (or lack thereof) she was creating that she was ready to make a change on every level.

She pruned her current assignment and moved back to Chicago, where she could work from home. She got her demo tapes back in circulation. Within one month, Eva got a call from someone who had downloaded her tape online. In the past, she had been very nervous in auditions. This time, her self-confidence was so strong, she nailed it. Eva became the voice-over for Sheryl Crow's commercials for Dell — a leap not just into the career of her dreams, but into a big-time national commercial. She had arrived.

LOOPS

Repeating the same patterns and drama from situation to situation, job to job, and relationship to relationship becomes an unconscious template for your life that leads to the lowest-energy choice of all.

Being on a roller coaster can be thrilling, but it's not viable as a long-term lifestyle choice. You're in a Loop when you have spent so much time in a Comfort Zone that it has become a pattern. The centrifugal force of habit keeps you there. Step off this ride and start to manage your energy in a way that moves you toward your goals. Otherwise, life itself may provide a wake-up call. When you stay in Loops, you re-create the same dramas and frustrations, no matter where you work or whom you marry.

The movie *Groundhog Day* is the ultimate example of a Loop. Bill Murray plays an obnoxious reporter who repeats the same frustrating day over and over until he breaks free by deciding to change his behavior. Each day, he changes one thing, gets one new result, and then gets to relive that new and improved day, only to face the next repeated behavior that wasn't working. It took many attempts, and it wasn't until he changed each part of this big Loop that he was able to get out of it.

WHY CHANGE?

While Comfort Zones can feel soothing and familiar, even if they're not good for you, Loops rarely feel okay. And it's more difficult to pull out of them. As you've probably heard, when you always do what you've always done, you'll always get what you've always gotten. When the pain you feel outweighs the fear of where you're going, you're ready to get out of the Loop. If you don't break these patterns and get out of the Loop, remember that life itself may get your attention in a dramatic fashion, something I refer to as a cosmic two-by-four: you get ill, you injure yourself, you're passed over for a promotion, or a friendship spontaneously combusts.

But just because you want to change doesn't mean you will. The centrifugal force of a Loop keeps you in it and makes it hard to change. If you keep wanting to go back to school or to buy your first home but always find a reason why you can't, you're feeling the force of a Loop. It takes a concerted effort to extricate yourself. Willpower is not enough. Understanding is the key.

Most of us are not addicts per se, but nearly everyone is addicted to certain behaviors, and we only change when we hit some sort of bottom. This awakening is different for everyone. For some, it can be enough to notice that their life isn't working and that they want a change. For others, it takes a major event like going bankrupt or experiencing another divorce. If you ignore the subtle adjustments, the two-by-four will hit harder until it has your full attention. Do not view this as good or bad. After all, without this adjustment, you would probably not have the opportunity to discover how you created your Loop in the first place.

THE OLD WAY OF DOING

Chances are you've experienced a number of Loops, unconsciously knocking your head against the wall over and over, feeling like a victim. You may say things like,

"Why does this always happen to me?"

"Life isn't fair."

"I can't believe my bad luck."

Or perhaps you blame outside circumstances and people for your Loops, generalizing with sentences like,

"There aren't any good men left."

"Kids today have no ambition."

"Management doesn't understand what employees need."

The old way is to feel at the mercy of life. The force feels so strong, it's as if you have no choice. Loops are customized to your psyche, your archetypes, and your blueprint. They are easier to see in hindsight than when you're in them. It's up to you to spot the trends. Every time I've been about to make a big career change, it's taken some huge turbulence to force me to take action and make the move. Because I learned at a very young age that I can overcome anything, I often stayed in a position far beyond the point that it was serving me. I wasn't focused on me. I was focused on beating the odds. I was going for the adrenaline rush. Ultimately, all I did was wear myself down.

Do you recognize these patterns in people you know? One man I worked with gets into a political fight with a co-worker every time he joins a new company. No matter where they live, the wife of a close friend complains that her neighbors are too gossipy. One of my college friends has repeatedly gained and lost the same fifty pounds her entire adult life. What is your pattern? Are you ready to change it?

THE NEW WAY OF BEING

Remember, the motion of the Loop keeps you in place. Because Loops contain emotional triggers, it takes the force of a conscious choice to get out. Here's how to do it:

1. Identify that you're in a Loop.

The first step in changing is to identify the Loop, and the best way to do that is to recognize the repetition and redundancy in your life. If you've tried several different approaches in getting close to your teenager, but she still seems distant, you're probably in a Loop. If you're angry with your second spouse for the same reasons you divorced the first, you're in a Loop. If you keep buying new golf equipment because you just can't find the right club, you're in a Loop.

Ask yourself,

- Do I keep getting the same result, no matter how hard I try?

- Do I feel as if I'm going nowhere?

- Are my frustration or my emotional issues now driving the situation?

- Am I feeling like a victim, that something is "being done" to me and there's nothing I can do to change it?

When you think about it, this is really pretty exciting. If something has clearly been dogging you your whole life, this is the chance to change it.

PLAYING THE FIELD

Describe a Loop you are currently in.
How long have you been in this Loop?
What is the centrifugal force keeping you there?

---

2. Look for assists.

In basketball, you can't score until your team is in position to make the shot. There's no such thing as a solo effort. The same is true of Loops. You need support in your court. Enlist the aid of a therapist, personal coach, spouse, sibling, parent, or friend.

The Field itself will assist from time to time in the form of redirection or opportunities that break the centrifugal force. The bigger the Loop, the bigger the redirection or adjustment the Field will give you. The assist may look like synchronicity. You wonder how to stop picking unreliable friends, and you hear about a book on this subject. Better yet, a reliable person shows up in your life and wants to be your friend. You decide to speak up at meetings, and the next day your boss suggests you join Toastmasters because he wants you to make more presentations.

Our friends can give us assists, yet sometimes it's hard to know when to listen and when to give advice. I recently stepped out of my Loop about this and was also able to assist my friend

Sarah in getting out of hers. Our mutual friend, Julie, was quite upset because her father was getting remarried less than a year after her mother had died. She sent some judgmental emails to Sarah and me, criticizing her father for marrying so soon. Sarah's father had become a widower three years earlier and remained single. Julie felt strongly that her father should be doing the same thing and enlisted Sarah's support.

In the past I would have thought, *Well, they think what they think. It's not my place to get involved.* This time I felt so strongly that I risked alienating them both. I wrote, "She's dead. She's gone. He's alone. How can we possibly know what he's going through? He was married for forty years, and now he's alone. It's his decision. He needs our love and support, not our judgment. Julie said she wished her dad could be as sensitive as yours, Sarah, and not remarry, but I've heard you say you'd give anything to see your dad happy again. You'd love for him to be remarried. So, what's everyone all worked up about? Let's get a reality check!"

Julie's reaction was lukewarm, but Sarah immediately called me.

"Wow! That was a real eye-opener for me. I didn't realize how much of this was projecting how bad I felt about losing my mom. It's not about Julie's dad at all."

Remember, you can ask for assists. Wendy had a small consulting company for twelve years, during which she Looped quite a few times over her finances. Her pattern was to spend time marketing and delivering her firm's services and paying scant attention to financial management until there was a crisis. She also had a pattern of feeling burdened by all her responsibilities and not seeing a way out. She felt as if the company were a huge weight she was dragging forward every day and didn't see a way to change the situation.

She knew she was in a Loop because she recognized the dire situation she was in once again, with negative cash flow, because of her high overhead. She met with Cheryl, her accountant, and asked her advice. Cheryl strongly suggested reducing what she paid for rent. Wendy still had two years on her lease and couldn't see any way to get out from under. After reflecting on this pattern of crisis, she decided to step out of her Loop and see what would happen. So she took the single step of calling her landlord.

"I see that the office next to ours is up for lease. If someone wants a bit more space, I'd be willing to give up half of mine," she said.

There was a slight pause, and then the landlord said, "Would you be willing to give up all of it?"

Wendy couldn't believe her ears. As it turned out, another tenant was scaling down and wanted a space exactly the size of Wendy's. Within a month the other tenant was in, Wendy was out, and her remaining employees were telecommuting happily from home. As she looked out at her rose garden one Tuesday morning, she felt absolutely ecstatic and more alive at work than she'd felt in years. All because she'd asked for an assist.

Notice when the Field sends some help, whether it's in the form of your accountant or a close friend's email.

PLAYING THE FIELD

Think of a time a friend pointed out one of your Loops.
What kind of assistance are you getting right now?
Think of a time a relative or spouse pointed out one of your Loops.
Did you resist? If so, was it because it hit a nerve?

3. Disengage.

Step back. Become the observer. If it weren't you but a close buddy in the Loop, how would you describe it, and what would you say? Become your own best friend. Provide the answers you'd give. The answers are within. Or, if you like, ask someone you trust. We can usually see Black Hole choices in others more easily than we do in ourselves. Chances are your friends can describe your Loops in detail.

Different people will need to disengage in different ways. The key is to get some distance from the challenge or Loop and try to see the circumstances or yourself in a new way, from a new perspective. Here's how my friend Patel did it. In a burst of self-reflection, he asked the six people who knew him best to list his greatest strengths and greatest weaknesses. He also wrote down his view of these areas, then looked for traits that appeared on two others' lists but not on his.

The positive trait that hadn't appeared on Patel's list was "generous." The negative trait was "stubborn." He acknowledged that he was often generous, but he flatly rejected the idea that he was stubborn. In fact, he felt angry that anyone could see him that way. And that is what's true of a Loop. You've been in it so long, you don't even know you're in it. The two people who had listed Patel's stubbornness, however, were his wife and his father. So he listened and accepted that it must be true, even though he couldn't see it. Within a week he caught himself becoming stubborn about something. He told me later this was a real eye-opener and had created an opportunity for him to get out of this Loop he'd been in for many years — probably since childhood.

The next time Patel got entrenched in his automatic

response of stubbornness with his wife, he stepped back and disengaged from that position. It allowed him to better understand his wife's point of view and how inbred his response to that situation was.

Remember, whatever you direct your energy toward will expand. So the very act of asking those near to you how they see you can shake your world. Once you put your request for personal feedback out there, you're responsible for managing what you get back. These are the big landmarks, the guideposts, the portals to big leaps. New results can be instantaneous, because now you're operating in the quantum field. That's the nature of the Field: what we focus on creates quantum leaps.

Right before you extract yourself from a Loop, the friction and the intensity build. Because you are hardwired to be in that Loop, you've worked up such momentum that your body, emotions, and memory don't want to let go. Why? Because we create many of these Loops in childhood, usually to keep us safe. We've all heard stories of people who hid their money in their houses because they lived through the Depression and didn't trust banks. Doing this helped them feel safe but ultimately didn't provide for their retirements the way investments might have. Or we've heard about people who grew up in highly critical home environments and as a result seem to constantly apologize for everything, unknowingly sabotaging their chances for respect and advancement. Loops are powerful. You are so wedged into that roller coaster seat, you really have to work to get out of it.

When you're getting ready to get off the roller coaster, the people around you will feel the change and may interact with you differently. People don't like change. If they've known you one way all your life, and you're redefining who you are, they'll resist. Right before you break out of a Loop it may feel as if the whole universe is saying, "You can't do this!" But you can.

FROM ONE LOOP TO ANOTHER

Loops can be annoying because you begin to feel that no matter what you do to change your circumstances, you keep getting the same unsatisfying results. Have you changed your situation but created the same Loop? I once walked away from an international position and made a huge career change, switching industries and moving to a company where I could create a more balanced lifestyle and work toward my dreams: writing this book and speaking about the Field. So what did I do? What I knew best: I started another Loop.

Many Loops begin in a Comfort Zone. I reverted to a Comfort Zone of keeping these hopes and dreams separate from my day-to-day business. I jumped to the conclusion that my new CEO would feel I wasn't fully committed to my day job if my goal was to do something other than increase profits and shareholder value. So I started Looping! And each Loop was bigger and more ambitious than the last. These Loops followed the pattern I was wired for, on a cellular level: overachievement. The first one was about needing more credentials, so I got a master's degree. Not just any master's degree. It had to be from a top-ten university.

When that was done, I started my second Loop, studying improv for a year and a half so I would feel more comfortable thinking on my feet before large crowds. Not just any improv training, but the mother of all improv training: the Players Workshop.

Then I joined the Secretan Center, an international organization on the cutting edge of bringing spirit and values into the workplace. I served on their board, volunteered my time, met some remarkable people, and invested money to lay the groundwork for my speaking career. Now that I'd accomplished all these imaginary imperatives, I was ready to write. But, when I sat down, nothing happened. I eventually shut down because of the many emotional agendas I had around success and failure. I lost all hope and started believing what people had been telling me all along: *You'll never get published. The speaker circuit is too competitive. Just write for the joy of writing.* I became deeply depressed. I had entered the Black Hole.

I jumped to the conclusion that because the book and the speaking circuit didn't happen when I thought they should have, I was a failure. To get myself out of the Black Hole, I reengaged in my job. When I was working full-throttle, back in the Power Zone, the ideas started flowing again. Now the time issue didn't matter. The words came.

I found the courage to break out of the Loop by telling the truth to my CEO, sharing that my real dream was to write and speak. Ironically, I became more valuable to my company because I had a skill they didn't know about that they needed. When I stopped Looping, I was able to give myself to my career without forgetting the real me. I was able to write and speak as part of my job, and the result is that you're holding this book in your hands today.

SUMMARY

- You Loop when you repeat the same patterns and dramas from situation to situation, job to job, and relationship to relationship.

- You're in a Loop when you have spent so much time in a Comfort Zone that it is now a pattern.

- When you stay in Loops, you re-create the same dramas and frustrations, no matter where you work or whom you marry.

- While Comfort Zones can feel soothing and familiar, even if they're not good for you, Loops never feel good. And it's more difficult to pull out of them than to pull out of a Comfort Zone.

- When the pain you feel outweighs your fear of where you're going, you're ready to get out of the Loop. If you don't break these patterns, remember that life itself may get your attention in a dramatic fashion: you get ill, you injure yourself, you're passed over for a promotion, a friendship spontaneously combusts.

- The centrifugal force of a Loop keeps you in it and makes it hard to change. Because Loops contain emotional triggers, it takes the force of a conscious choice to get out.

- Identify that you're in a Loop. Ask yourself, *Do I keep getting the same result, no matter what I try? Do I feel as if I'm going nowhere?*

- Look for assists. If it seems appropriate, enlist the aid of a therapist or personal coach.

- Disengage. Step back. Become the observer. If it weren't you but a close buddy in the Loop, how would you describe it, and what would you say?

- Right before you extract yourself from a Loop, the friction and the intensity start to build. You've worked up such momentum that your body, emotions, and cellular memory don't want to let go.

- When you're getting ready to get off the roller coaster, the people around you may resist. Do it anyway.

CHAPTER SIX

MAGNETS

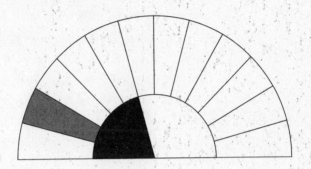

Why is it that when you really worry about something and try with all your might to avoid it, it still happens? Have you ever used positive affirmations without any results? Perhaps you have a strong intention that is not coming to fruition. You're not stuck in a Comfort Zone. You're not lost in a Head Trip. You're not in a Loop. And yet, what you want still isn't happening. Why? A Magnet is at work. This chapter will explain Magnets, how they operate and how you can move beyond their powerful pull.

Magnets often have an ominous feel about them because they are the consequence of operating in the Fear Zone for extended periods. Magnets don't just appear out of nowhere. They take shape so gradually that most likely you won't even be aware you've created one. And they often take time to discover. The following story demonstrates the complexity of Magnets and how they're created.

Everything about my friend Debi screams that she should be married and a mother. She is the warmest and most empathetic person you would ever want to meet. She has a high-powered job yet is down-to-earth and kind, completely devoted to her parents and siblings. Attractive and extraordinarily successful, she has had many relationships and many proposals, but they have never led to marriage. At the end of each relationship, she walked away feeling she was not good enough, and at fifty she was still single.

After thirty frustrating years of relationships that did not lead to marriage, Debi had had enough pain, enough wasted time, and enough reflection. She was ready to face what was really going on. With a little help from a supportive friend, Debi found the courage to look deeply into herself, and then it became clear: when she was very young, under some very difficult circumstances, she'd had an abortion. This choice had stayed with her, and Debi brought the pain of it into every relationship. In a flash, Debi realized that she was the one who thought she wasn't good enough, and that's why she only brought men into her life who found her unworthy. With this revelation, Debi felt as if the weight of the world had been suddenly lifted from her shoulders, and she decided that she had to forgive herself once and for all. Within weeks of this epiphany, she met the man who would become her husband.

Magnets don't just happen to you. You create them. When you immerse yourself in shame, fear, and negativity, you charge them with power. Even though Debi had wanted with all her heart to be married, the Magnet was more powerful. It's a slippery slope when you're operating in the Fear Zone of the Energy Spectrum. If you spend much of your time Head Tripping, you'll create Loops. If you constantly Loop, you'll create Magnets. And Magnets draw in all your fears, sending you even further into the Black Hole.

Low-energy choices are more seductive than high-energy ones, and Magnets are the lowest of the low. Perhaps you've used affirmations and visualizations. You've taped a card to your mirror and repeat something like this every morning:

I am happy and successful.

The right career is coming to me.

I am radiantly healthy.

You may remember Stuart Smalley, Al Franken's character on *Saturday Night Live*. He was famous for repeating, "I'm good enough, I'm smart enough, and doggone it, people like me!" The way he said this, it really didn't seem as if he felt good enough or smart enough, and when he was through, all you liked about him was laughing at him. Words are not enough. If you have Magnets attached to your intentions, the Magnets will prevail. Affirmations have gotten a bad rap. "You can't wish your way to success," say the critics. And they're partially correct. Affirmations don't always work when you attach fear to them because the fear will drown them out. It's more than just saying words. You must back them up with a powerful feeling. You must infuse the words with your energy. Otherwise, your Magnets will prevail over your affirmations.

MAGNETS

Your negative, fear-based beliefs can actually create what you're most trying to avoid.

Because negative thoughts require less conscious awareness than positive thoughts, they spread much more quickly. On days when you're predisposed to low-energy thinking, you will hear more complaining than celebration, more criticism than praise. Why? Because you're focusing on validating that perspective, and what you focus on expands.

When you've been operating in the Fear Zone, you are very vulnerable to low-energy thinking and low-energy actions. It helps to be conscious of this dynamic. When you're stuck on the left end of the Energy Spectrum, it's like trudging through mud. Every step takes so much energy. And the more Magnets and Black Holes you have in your life, the more predisposed you will be to more of the same. It's like having a weakened immune system. Eventually, you get a cold — or worse.

Magnets are the most complex and ironic of all the energetic choices because they operate in reverse, and you're not always aware of how you're summoning to you the last thing in the world you want. For example, if you believe *I'll always be in debt. I have so many bills. But I really want financial freedom*, you probably will stay in debt forever. Why?

Let's break this down. If you believe you'll always be in debt, you will. This statement is the Magnet. *I have so many bills* is also a Magnet. *I really want financial freedom* expresses the desire in your intention, but it is expressed as wanting. When you focus on the wanting, the Field gives you exactly that — the wanting — instead of the result. What you intended as a statement of affirmation is really a three-pronged Magnet.

Let's take another example. If you think *I hate my job, but it sure would be better if I got that promotion*, then you're likely to have a long and miserably successful career. *I hate my job* acts as a huge Magnet because low-energy emotions are immensely powerful and fuel Magnets. Hate is an extremely strong emotion and dominates the second half of your statement, *it sure would be better if I got that promotion.* You can't be in a low-energy place and create a high-energy opportunity. You're asking the Field to create a duality. Your negative thoughts about your job will overpower any thought of success or promotion. Magnets invite you to look at how you view yourself in the world and to recognize the incongruent thoughts that interfere with your goals.

WHY CHANGE?

Without an understanding of Magnets, it can seem as if other people have easy lives in which everything unfolds for them, while you walk around with a rain cloud over your head. You think bad things are being done to you instead of realizing you had a hand in them. When you create Magnets, you give up your power. The negative energy of low-energy choices consumes and debilitates you more quickly and more completely than any other emotion. All low-energy choices come from fear, and Magnets are the mother of all fear-based choices. They are the quickest way into the Black Hole. With each relationship, my friend Debi felt even worse about herself. Her feeling of unworthiness fueled the Magnet. After many years of operating that way, she fell into the Black Hole. Yet Debi could not have come to her Breakthrough without first going through the Black Hole.

When you expose yourself repeatedly to fear-induced, painful thoughts, the Magnet gets bigger, and as it gets bigger, its pull on you becomes stronger. You lose your sense of self and give up your power because you're feeding the Magnet, not yourself.

THE OLD WAY OF DOING

Like other low-energy choices, Magnets create a victim mentality and encourage blaming, but they do so even more powerfully. Some people attempt to muscle the Magnet. Others ignore it, hoping it will go away, and more than a few people give up and give in, feeling they're somehow doomed.

You can't simply overcome or overpower a Magnet without identifying it and understanding why it exists. Let's go back to our earlier example. A person who wants financial freedom might read a book about it, take a money management class, and hire an investment advisor. But because there are underlying Magnets in his intention, financial freedom will remain elusive. He will continue to try other options: joining Debtors Anonymous, setting up and following a budget, and buying Quicken to track his spending. He maintains a hopeful attitude. But no matter how committed he is in mind and action, the Magnet prevails. Don't underestimate its pull. A Magnet can be very alluring because it's much easier to feel bad about yourself than it is to consciously move to another place on the Energy Spectrum.

You know you're in the pull of a Magnet when no matter how hard you try or how good your intentions are, you're not getting what you want. Once you've identified a Magnet, the next step is to understand why it exists. In Debi's case, her sense of unworthiness that festered for thirty years was the cause. But until she understood the source of her problem, it was easy to blame it on the fact that there just weren't any good men out there; that she just wasn't thin, pretty, or young enough; that her success intimidated men; or that it was her fate to be single. Once she realized she was helping to create these results, she instantly neutralized her Magnet.

THE NEW WAY OF BEING

Although Magnets are one of the most challenging low-energy choices, the good news is that they present your biggest opportunity for personal insight and change. Discovering and uncovering your Magnets can deliver the equivalent of five years of therapy in an instant. As with other low-energy choices, it's important not to judge. You've created the Magnet for a reason. Why waste valuable energy blaming and judging? Remember, Magnets are an incredible teacher — if you can be conscious of how and when they show up in your life.

Regular magnets can lose their magnetic field in various ways. A sharp blow will sometimes do it, depending on the material. Some materials simply lose most of their magnetism over time because of molecular migration. However, Magnets seldom lose *all* their power. In physics this is called hysteresis. In life, sometimes Magnets lose their power over time. Sometimes an event that feels like a sharp blow motivates us to make a change. But Magnets can always gain their full power back, plus some. This process can make you feel hysterical if you are not aware of the role Magnets are playing in your life.

Discovering and neutralizing your Magnets takes time. It's not a quick process, but the results can happen in a flash.

Remember, the Field operates differently than your hierarchy at work or your structure at home. It's not on the same time line. This is not about making it perfect and solving the problem forever; it's about your awareness of how you create and cope with your Magnets. Though the outcome can be wonderful, when you're stuck to a Magnet, it can feel awful. Here's how to unstick yourself:

1. Identify what scares you most.

Name something you really want that is not developing in your life. You stayed in a Head Trip, it evolved into a Loop, and now it's a full-fledged Magnet. Perhaps it's career success. Or becoming physically fit. Or having harmony at home. Here's a helpful hint: think about a lifelong issue. If you contemplate long enough, you'll discover a Magnet.

PLAYING THE FIELD

What scares you most?
Describe it in detail.
What is your earliest memory of this fear?

2. Look for any contradictory views when stating your goal.

What kinds of Fear Zone words and phrases do you hear yourself saying about this part of your life? Look at the decisions you're making and their repercussions. If this is too difficult, ask someone who knows you well. Your Magnets are very obvious to those around you. We've all known people who say they always have bosses who don't respect them. Or that they're always getting ripped off by someone. Or perhaps it's a more obvious personal pattern, like constantly being a day late and a dollar short. What do your friends notice about you?

PLAYING THE FIELD

When you read over your description of your goal, do you see any contradictions? If so, is it clear now what your Magnet is?

---

3. Ask, "How could this be holding me back?"

Look at how this contradictory view is showing up in your life. What habits have you formed around it or in avoidance of it? What choices have you made because of it? Look for mixed messages. When fear is the focal point in the wish to change, news flash: it's not going to happen until you address the fear, the most powerful part of the Magnet. If you hate your job but get that promotion mentioned earlier, you'll find new ways to hate your job. What do you dislike about your job? The way you're viewed? The type of work you do? Your boss? The hours? The location? The commute? Break it down.

4. Ask yourself, "What can I do from my base of power to change this situation?"

Start internally. Identify three steps you can take to address the Magnet, then take them. A regular magnet is powerless when you decharge it. That's what you do to an energetic Magnet when you break it down. Action moves you into the

Power Zone. Once you master a Magnet on this level, you can look at this phenomenon in all parts of your life, like health and fitness, your home, and your creativity.

For a long time, Amanda had worked directly with the president of a company. After eighteen years, the company decided that the purchasing department would handle all their vendor contracts, so she was no longer able to meet with the president and instead was directed to meet with Grace, the company's meeting planner. She was worried about losing her base of power and working at this lower level in the organization. She felt diminished, and her ego was bruised. In fact, she carried this low energy into the meeting. Grace picked up on it and was so surprised at Amanda's negativity that she actually asked why their company had done business with her for so long.

This unstuck Amanda from the Magnet she was creating, and she quickly went to neutral. She realized her ego had caused much of this problem and that she had created a Magnet. She immediately began to focus on creating a connection with Grace and was able to neutralize the Magnet before it affected her business with other clients and became a self-fulfilling prophecy.

PLAYING THE FIELD

Describe a time when one of your Magnets became more powerful because of the fear you fed it.
What could you have done from your base of power to neutralize it?

Ironically, when I first introduced the concept of Magnets to my speaking audiences, I created a huge one. I was very worried because this topic is so complex. *What if they don't understand the concept? What if I can't get it across?* That led to *What if they don't like me?* I was sliding down the slippery slope of the Fear Zone. What happened? I got in front of an audience pivotal to my future success, the Magnet kicked in, and I bombed. I felt so devastated that I fell into a Black Hole and stopped doing presentations and working on my book.

Finally I confronted the Magnet.

What scares me the most? I asked myself. *Failing. This topic is so important and so complex. I want to tell the world about it, but I'm afraid I can't adequately explain it. What's holding me back? I tried, and I failed.*

For me, the classic overachiever, this felt like death. I was holding the conflicting view that I wanted to tell the world about Magnets but couldn't adequately explain the concept. I couldn't see this at first and spent months in a Black Hole. Once I realized how I had created it, the Magnet was out in the open, and I returned to my base of power and took action, creating more speaking opportunities. At a conference in Miami two years later, I gave this presentation again and was the highest-rated speaker. I neutralized that Magnet, and now I speak all over the world.

Because working on Magnets is so intense, I often wear a special bracelet my sister gave me that helps me view Magnets in a lighthearted way. I had been living in the Fear Zone for a couple of weeks with family and job struggles, hadn't been working out or eating right, and felt fat. I knew that operating in the Fear Zone predisposed me to Magnets, but I just couldn't snap out of it and was having a rocky morning. I felt terribly self-conscious as I waited for forty-five minutes in the hotel's fancy restaurant for my breakfast appointment to arrive. In my diminished state, I was sure that everyone was staring at me.

Just look like you belong, I told myself. *Be comfortable*. But nothing worked. The tension was only increasing, and I felt the Magnet's pull.

As I casually reached for my glass of orange juice, the magnetic clasp on my bracelet caused my knife to suddenly jump up off the table and affix itself onto the bracelet, knocking the glass over. Then everyone truly was staring. Though mortified, I had to laugh. The power of my low-energy thinking had activated Magnets on two levels that morning, creating the attention I so feared! I smile every time I wear that bracelet because it reminds me how powerful I really can be.

Now that we've reviewed the four low-energy choices of the Fear Zone, let's move on to exploring the six high-energy choices of the Power Zone.

SUMMARY

- Your negative, fear-based beliefs can actually create what you're most trying to avoid.

- Magnets don't just happen to you. You create them. When you immerse yourself in fear and negativity, you charge them with power.

- Overindulging in any low-energy choices will make you vulnerable to Magnets.

- Magnets are the most complex and ironic of all the energetic choices because they operate in reverse, and you're not always aware of how you're summoning to you the last thing you want.

- Magnets are the quickest way to the Black Hole. When you expose yourself repeatedly to fear-induced, painful thoughts, the Magnet gets bigger, and as it gets bigger, its ability to pull on you grows stronger.

- You can't overcome or overpower a Magnet without first understanding why it exists.

- Discovering and uncovering your Magnet can deliver the equivalent of five years of therapy in an instant.

- Identify what scares you most. Part of this process involves understanding who and what you can and cannot control.

- Ask, "How could this be holding me back?" Look at the decisions you make because of this fear and the repercussions of these decisions. Ask yourself, "What can I do from my base of power?" Start internally. Identify three steps you can take, and then take them.

PART THREE

THE POWER ZONE AND ITS SIX HIGH-ENERGY CHOICES

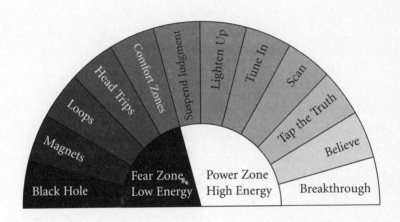

CHAPTER SEVEN

SUSPEND JUDGMENT

Have you ever held a strong opinion about a person or situation, only to discover that you were completely wrong? This chapter explains the limiting role that judgment plays in our lives and how, when we learn to Suspend Judgment, a world of Breakthroughs opens up. The story below shows just how easy it is to jump to the wrong conclusions.

Gillian had splurged on a beautiful red-and-gold brocade designer sofa. It was the most she had ever spent on a piece of furniture, but the sofa perfectly suited her turn-of-the-century brownstone. When she moved into a more contemporary home, the sofa no longer fit, and because it was so large she had to store it in her garage.

Peter, the contractor who was working on her home, misunderstood the situation, and when a delivery was being made, he gave the sofa to the man driving the truck. When Gillian returned and heard what had happened, she was beside herself. Though she might have considered selling the sofa, she certainly didn't want to give it away. Peter felt terrible and agreed to track down the driver, who explained that he could not afford to offer any payment for the sofa right then. Gillian went into a Head Trip: *He is taking advantage, he knows I have no way to get the sofa back and has me over a barrel, so he's pushing a hard bargain.*

Peter felt so bad that he offered to retrieve the sofa on his own time. Gillian stopped and considered. *Why am I so angry? It was just sitting in my garage and doesn't fit in my house. I don't have time for the hassle of selling it. Maybe it was meant to be with the truck driver.* She told Peter to let the driver have it and to enjoy it. Later that day Gillian learned that the driver was incredibly grateful. He said his wife had been fighting cancer, that all their money had gone to paying the medical bills, and that he was able to give her the couch for Valentine's Day. She loved it. Gillian was very pleased.

SUSPEND JUDGMENT

Letting go of your interpretations of and opinions about others, outcomes, and especially yourself will immediately take you out of the Fear Zone of low-energy choices and expand your possibilities.

We all make hundreds of judgments every day and seldom get the direct feedback that they are mostly inaccurate. When you make a judgment, you arrive at a conclusion based on reason, discernment, evaluation, and comparison. We've all jumped to wrong conclusions or made false interpretations or judged people based on a first impression. Gillian had never met the truck driver and automatically assumed he was trying to take advantage of her. And she was wrong. Think about how you do this. You don't know someone. You've never even met him, but you know his reputation, or, if it's a co-worker, you've heard about various projects he's been involved with. Maybe he works with a colleague or a friend of yours. And you definitely have some judgments about him (sometimes you call these opinions or facts). Does it make sense to do this?

Still, most of us reserve our harshest or most critical judgments for ourselves. For example, we judge how quickly or effectively we handle situations we've never experienced before. But learning and mastery come in a sequence, and you cannot skip from A to Z. Remember when you learned your ABCs? When I was in kindergarten, Mrs. Seidenkranz taught us a new section of the alphabet each day. Every morning I couldn't wait to get to school and learn the next sequence of letters. I had no way of monitoring my performance. I didn't know how much more there was to learn, so I didn't judge or evaluate the process or myself. I just liked singing the ABC song. My focus was on learning and having fun.

Research done by UCLA professor of education Marilyn Kourilsky shows that 97 percent of kindergartners think out of the box, while only 3 percent of people by the age of thirty do.[1] Wouldn't it be great if you could still bring such enthusiasm to every day? The reason you close off is that you've been battered by a lifetime of premature evaluations made by you and others. A business consultant once told me that every new idea she has is typically met with nine different criticisms. The excitement has been stomped out of us. As a result, the first reaction most of us have to a situation is often judgment or criticism.

Do you judge yourself if you don't do something right the first time? If you're like most people, you have harsh inner voices that criticize nearly everything you do. You hear these sometimes in an unguarded moment:

You made a poor decision.
You should have known better.
You could have done better.

The next time you hear that nagging inner judge, extend the same courtesy to yourself that you would to friends making negative comments about themselves and tell yourself to stop.

WHY CHANGE?

Suspending Judgment is the gateway skill of the Power Zone. This choice will help get you out of the Fear Zone, where you most likely ended up after making some sort of negative judgment. Suspending Judgment opens up other possibilities and saves you a huge amount of upset and stress. It is also one of the best ways to stay out of the Black Hole. No matter how dire a situation appears, if you resist the urge to attach too quickly to a position, you allow for the possibility that it might not be so bad and that perhaps even great things may result.

Perhaps you have to find a new day-care provider and feel upset about this change for your child, only to find you're both thrilled with the new situation. Or maybe you've faced an involuntary reorganization or job transfer that turned out better than you could have imagined. A friend of mine in California was once laid off from a software company and doubled her income two years later in a position she probably never would have looked for if her first job had continued.

The more you Suspend Judgment, the more peaceful your life will become. You'll feel much more philosophical and less emotionally addicted to life's normal ups and downs. This is not to be confused with losing your edge. In fact, you'll be working the exponentially powerful Energy Edge, because you'll be able to think more clearly, with less emotional charge. By Suspending Judgment you move to a higher frequency, where every action has more power, and you will directly benefit from the Energy Edge. You'll be unclouded by fear and upset and will move toward gaining new wisdom. You'll enjoy life more when you Suspend Judgment because you won't be limited by all your opinions. You'll also waste less energy becoming upset. Remember how angry Gillian was and how much energy she directed toward judging? The real story turned out to be completely different from what she had imagined.

Suspending Judgment is perhaps the most important high-energy choice because it opens the door to possibilities you can't imagine. Suspending Judgment stops a downward spiral before it begins and allows you to make more powerful, and less obvious, choices. You'll tap into the Field and experience frequent creative breakthroughs, better one-on-one relationships, and less negativity in your life. Your broader perspective will give you better balance. Both on and off the job, your actions will be congruent with your intentions. As a result, you will feel more energy at the end of the day and be far less likely to burn out.

When you Suspend Judgment, you allow for many options you haven't even considered. Let go of all your ideas about life as usual and open yourself to a new perspective, at home and at work. Detaching but still participating, you'll know when to put your mind in neutral instead of pressing the gas and throwing it into fifth gear.

THE OLD WAY OF DOING

Life as usual for most of us includes opinions about those we encounter and interpretations of events that stay fixed in our minds. When you make a judgment, you unconsciously set into motion a certain chain of events. You tap into the Field without realizing it, sending your energy into directions you may not actually want them to go in. A conclusion means an end point. No more processing. No more possibility. Once you make a judgment, you become attached to a certain approach, limiting the possible results. Things aren't always what they seem, and when you lock into one point of view, you close the door to other opportunities.

When you jump to conclusions, charging full speed ahead and inventing more rules and regulations, all based on control, then you're making low-energy choices.

THE NEW WAY OF BEING

When we Suspend Judgment, we gain access to all the other high-energy choices. Because judging is what we naturally do as human beings, this behavior change can feel formidable.

With practice, you'll notice yourself easing up more and more quickly. Here are some ways to develop this skill:

1. Suspend Judgment on others.

When I was in my thirties, I lived in Laguna Beach, California. One morning I left for work and took the same route I always did to I-5. I was driving about forty miles an hour, when suddenly a blue Honda whipped out in front of me from a mall parking lot. I slammed on the brakes and almost went up onto the center island, into a tree. My heart was racing. I barely avoided colliding with the car. When I looked over, all I could see was the backside of the woman's head as she drove away. I couldn't believe it. No wave. No nod. Absolutely no acknowledgment that she had almost caused an accident!

This incident bothered me all day. Besides feeling shaken, I was also amazed that the driver had driven away so brazenly. It was like a slap in the face. *How could anyone be so inconsiderate? Even if she didn't see me when she pulled out, I know she saw me after she made me jump lanes.* By the end of the day I had this woman all figured out. She was insensitive, uncaring, and self-absorbed. Not to mention the fact that she was a lousy driver. Boy, did I have her number! And to make matters worse, she had ruined my day.

I got home around 7:00 that night and parked my car in the same spot I always did, in a carport near my apartment. I felt crabby and couldn't wait for the day to be over. The next morning, as I was about to pull out of my parking spot, I saw a note under my windshield wiper. It said:

I am the woman who pulled out in front of you this morning. I can't tell you how sorry I am. I looked before I

pulled out and did not see you. You were in my blind spot.
After it happened, I saw you were okay and drove off out
of embarrassment. I felt bad all day and couldn't believe
my luck when I came home and recognized your car in the
lot next to mine. Please accept my apologies.
Your neighbor

I was stunned. I had squandered a whole day in the darkness of the Black Hole, thinking nasty things about her. And
I'd made sure I told everyone the story, too, trying to pull
them into the Black Hole as well with my drama and negativity. After all was said and done, I realized how wrong I had
been and how absurd my behavior had been. Though it's normal to be upset about a close call, I had chosen to direct my
upset at the other driver and had made it all about her.

PLAYING THE FIELD

Think of a time you jumped to a conclusion.
How did it alter your day?

2. Suspend Judgment on outcomes.

Reality is not always what it seems. How many times have
you come to a conclusion without having all the information?
My friend Linda McCallum calls this *premature evaluation*, and
you know how embarrassing that can be! Premature evaluations happen in the blink of an eye. They're so automatic, you
don't realize what you've set in motion.

George, a widower after forty-three years of marriage, told
me recently, "I always accused my wife of moving things when

I couldn't find them. Now I'm realizing I absentmindedly put objects in different places. I guess it was me all that time. When I think of all the years we argued over something so stupid that turned out to be my fault anyway, it makes me sad."

Over the years, I've noticed my neighbor Douglas making a similar premature evaluation about Donna, his cleaning lady. One morning he couldn't find his keys and felt upset that Donna had moved them from the place he usually keeps them on the wall. Exasperated, he searched his kitchen drawers for a spare set of keys and finally left for work. As he opened the door, he was surprised to find his keys still dangling in the lock. He'd gone inside and to bed the night before and left them hanging there.

Like me, you have probably grown up being trained to think right and wrong, good and bad. From the perspective of the quantum field, these are only two of many possible realities and severely limit your view. Be careful not to judge the Black Hole as bad and Breakthrough as good because this also launches you into premature evaluations instead of allowing you to experience what is happening right in front of you. Have you ever fought really hard to get something, without succeeding, only to realize that your failure was actually a blessing in disguise? I was once on a team that went after a prestigious $60 million piece of business in the New York banking industry. The entire process took more than a year. We made it with one other company to the final cut. So much preparation and hard work had gone into winning this new client that we felt devastated when we were designated backup supplier instead of primary.

We and the other company had both priced the business competitively and lowered our margins drastically in exchange for large volumes of revenue. Later, the client went through some huge cutbacks and didn't live up to the revenue projections that formed the pricing structure. Our competitor never made money from the deal. On the other hand, as backup supplier with higher margins, we didn't lose money, and we kept our foot in the door for the next bid after the client had recovered from its woes.

This reminds me of one of my favorite parables, which goes something like this: a farmer had a son who ran away from home, and everyone said, "That's bad." And then the son returned with a horse he had found, and everyone said, "That's good!" Then the son fell off the horse and broke his leg, and everyone said, "That's bad." But then, when war broke out, the boy could not go into battle, and everyone said, "That's good!"

And so the story goes. The point is, there is no end, and based on where you're at in the story, your perception changes. That's the risk of premature evaluation: you waste your time and energy on something that may not even be true. The reason for something may become clear later, or it might not.

PLAYING THE FIELD

When did you make a judgment that a situation was negative, only to have it turn out positive?
What other aspects of your life were affected by your premature evaluation?

3. Suspend Judgment on yourself.

If you can Suspend Judgment on others, you need to be able to do the same for yourself. Here's an example of how one woman did it. Patrice had wanted a second child for a long time. She and her husband had waited eight years for their first child, and another eight years passed before she became pregnant again. Joe arrived nearly three months prematurely and only lived for one week.

Patrice went into the Blackest Hole of her life. She was only able to move out of this Black Hole by attaching to something larger than herself. She became very clear that her mission was to find a troubled child whom no one else wanted. Patrice and her family embarked on the lengthy adoption process of research, interviews, paperwork, and setting up their support system. Aaron came into their life right before Thanksgiving that year. A crack baby who had been removed from his birth home, he suffered from ADHD, ADD, and various chemical imbalances. He had lived in eight different foster homes.

It was immediately clear that Aaron would be a real handful. He was prone to violent outbursts and was always getting into trouble at school. Their efforts to manage Aaron challenged Patrice's relationship with her husband as well as their relationship with their older son, who became withdrawn and ill and missed a significant number of school days. The financial strain caused by Aaron's medical needs increased. So did the violence. Patrice felt she was failing her family.

Realizing she might have to give up Aaron, Patrice had to Suspend Judgment on herself about failing her family and failing this child she thought she was meant to adopt. After she reflected on it, she realized that she was not meant to have him forever. Counselors felt he would do better in a home where he would be an only child. Along came a single man in his late twenties from Rhode Island, a social worker who counseled troubled children and was looking for a child of his own. Patrice later told me, "All this time I thought I was a failure. What I learned was that I was keeping Aaron safe and holding him until the person meant to be with him long-term would be available." Patrice had made the premature evaluation that she was a failure when, in fact, she had given her son exactly what he needed.

Should is a low-energy word. Eliminate it from your vocabulary — especially in reference to yourself. Don't be so tyrannical about how you ought to react to a situation. When you make a mistake, learn from it, and then let go of the emotional charge. You seldom know the whole story, especially its outcome, while it is taking place. That is why it is so important to let go of premature evaluations — especially when you're in the Fear Zone.

PLAYING THE FIELD

Think of a time when you judged yourself very harshly. When you shift your focus from judgment to learning, what happens?

GOING TO NEUTRAL

When I was sixteen, my cousin Gayle taught me how to use a manual transmission just after I got my driver's license. I had great difficulty managing the gears in her cool red five-speed. I confused first and fourth, and I could never find reverse. I quickly learned that the easiest way to find the right gear was to go to neutral. Though it added a step, it helped me get to the next gear more smoothly.

That's the key to overcoming premature evaluation. Instead of jumping to an opinion, go to neutral. Going to neutral keeps you open to another perspective. No doubt you've already experienced this:

- in an argument with your spouse or child when you both take a time-out;
- in brainstorming meetings, where all ideas are welcome;
- when you've given someone the benefit of the doubt;
- when you've refused to spread gossip;
- when you've waited to make a decision until you had all the facts;
- when you haven't blamed the messenger.

If things don't go your way and you're able to be in the unknown for a while, you create the space you need to get to resolution quickly. If you feel angry that your teenager didn't make curfew last night, you're probably not going to create much family harmony at dinner tonight. When you go to neutral, you can function again and find the right gear to move you in the right direction.

We all get triggered into judgments every day by what we hear, see, and think. Each time, you have a choice: Do you go directly into action, or do you go to neutral? One of the quickest ways to go to neutral is simply to observe your initial emotional reaction to a situation. Ask, *What aspect of me is being triggered?* Listen to that dialogue the way you'd listen to your best friend pouring her heart out to you.

These Fear Zone triggers aren't going to go away, but they'll settle down if you acknowledge them. The choices in the Fear Zone operate at such a low frequency on the Energy Spectrum that you cannot transcend them. All the light and love you throw at the Fear Zone are incapable of shifting it. Acceptance is the answer. As I heard David R. Hawkins once say, "No matter how nice you are to a Komodo dragon, it will always eat you."

Look at aspects of yourself in the same way. It's not your job to transform them. It's your job to listen to and accept them. When you do that, you go to neutral with the power of all of you. Your frequency goes up when you accept all those multiple realities of you, and these include the low-energy realities. By acknowledging and accepting the Fear Zone aspects of yourself, your own frequency instantly rises. Ironically, that is the moment when you will transcend! In the 1930s, Erwin Schrödinger's physics experiments confirmed that we can't observe or measure an object without affecting it or ourselves. Therefore, even if you don't know the solution to a problem, if you can at least observe the reaction you're having to it (e.g., being a hothead), you can affect the situation. When you become conscious of the emotional charge of a situation, you're no longer being run by it, and often the emotion itself will dissipate.

This detached state of observation is key. Throughout the day, you will experience many emotions, which is normal. But if a particular emotion is disproportionate to the situation, know you've been triggered and acknowledge that. Focus on the emotional charge and identify it (e.g., anger, fear, sadness).

Then get out of your head by taking some deep breaths, walking, drinking water, or eating some kind of food that grounds you. If you are physically constrained, like in a meeting or on a plane, push away from the desk or get up from your seat. Then let the situation go. Mentally set it to the side. Most of us respond to our initial emotion and jump right into some action. Resist this urge. Go to neutral instead.

Psychologist Gabriele Hilberg once told me, "Don't pay attention to the first thing a person does. Pay attention to the second." When you are willing to go to neutral and Suspend Judgment on your boss, your co-workers, your family, your spouse, your friends, strangers who cross your path, and even people you read about in the newspaper, you will open up to the higher frequencies. You are opening the door to all the other high-energy choices and all the potential they offer.

If you choose to stay in your emotions, reliving old stories and triggers, you'll make more judgments. The Blame Game (a low-energy pastime) seems to be part of everyday life, but when you use your energy by blaming, it shifts everything, taking you out of neutral and into emotion. Notice and step back into neutral. Your husband doesn't remember your anniversary. You feel slighted and resentful. You can notice this reaction and come to the premature evaluation that he doesn't really care, and that if you meant anything to him, he would have acknowledged you on this special day. Or, you can choose to stop after you notice the emotion. We all feel disappointment at times, and while this is a normal emotion, the act of nonjudgment allows you to go to neutral, and then to move on the Energy Spectrum into higher-energy choices because the emotional charge is gone. Suspending Judgment provides the opportunity to see a situation in a way that wouldn't have occurred to you. It can even feel miraculous. Try this for a week and experience the results for yourself.

Think of situations that trigger an automatic response in you.
How might these situations change if you go to neutral?

BARKING UP THE RIGHT TREE

Last spring my friend Lupe noticed that someone had hit the small tree in front of her house. Part of its bark was missing, and the tree was leaning toward the sidewalk, whacking pedestrians as they walked by. She couldn't imagine what had happened, since the tree was nearly three feet from the street. One day, her neighbor remarked that the tree trimmers who had worked on Lupe's property during the winter had hit it when they backed their cherry picker between the houses.

Lupe called Mike, the owner of the company, told him what had happened, and asked him to stake up the tree. After they had exchanged a few voice mails, he came over in person and vehemently denied that his men had hit the tree. "At that point," Lupe told me, "I decided to get off it. Even though it made sense that the cherry picker had hit it, perhaps my neighbor was wrong. At any rate, I didn't want to invest another minute of worrying about it." She told Mike that she believed him, and he left.

Three weeks later, Mike came to her door with his crew. He apologized, and it was clear he felt bad. It turned out that his crew had hit the tree and had told him, but he'd forgotten. And when he'd double-checked with the supervisor, he'd received incorrect information. (Lupe wondered if this reminder happened after Mike had prematurely evaluated her and complained to his crew about the crazy lady who'd called him!) Five apologies later, they departed. "It felt satisfying to solve the mystery," Lupe reported, "but what was even more gratifying was the decision I had made earlier to Suspend Judgment. I had enjoyed three weeks of peace, rather than resentment, and I felt equally peaceful when they set the record straight because I had gotten to use my time for high-energy activities, instead of obsessing, complaining, and repeating the story to everyone I knew." If you learn how to go to neutral, you will experience a more peaceful and powerful life too.

SUMMARY

- Suspending Judgment is the gateway skill of the Power Zone. This choice will help get you out of the Fear Zone, where you most likely ended up after making some sort of negative judgment.

- Suspending Judgment prevents you from going into the Black Hole because it allows you to make more powerful, and less obvious, choices.

- You'll enjoy life more when you Suspend Judgment because you won't be limited by all your opinions. You'll also waste less energy becoming upset.

- Suspend Judgment on others.

- Suspend Judgment on outcomes.

- Suspend Judgment on yourself.

- Go to neutral. One of the quickest ways is simply to observe your initial emotional reaction to a situation.

- Be careful not to judge the Black Hole as bad and Breakthrough as good, because doing this also launches you into premature evaluations instead of allowing you to experience what is happening right in front of you.

CHAPTER EIGHT

LIGHTEN UP

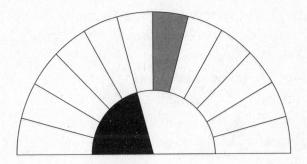

Have you ever been so stressed out, feeling yourself quickly slipping into the Fear Zone of the Energy Spectrum — and then you decided to laugh at your situation? Or have you ever been so stressed that you broke out into laughter at what seemed a really inappropriate time? Whether you choose laughter or the laughter chooses you, always choose to Lighten Up. This chapter explores how this small shift in energy can yield big results by instantly popping you back into the Power Zone.

When we are taking ourselves most seriously is when we most need to Lighten Up. I once had an office on the mezzanine level of the Marriott on Michigan Avenue in Chicago. This was an unusual and enjoyable place to work. I was surrounded by retail shops, which made the walk to the restroom a great distraction.

The Korean lady who owned the import shop down the hall from me had a Pekingese dog that always wore ribbons in his hair and was crazy about me. When I passed this store I would step in to pet my little friend. He would bark like mad and dance around. One particularly intense Monday I dashed out of my office to use the restroom. On my way back, I took a minute to stop and pet the dog. As I left, he flew out the door, yipping madly, and trailed me down the hall.

"Don't follow me," I said to him, as if that would do any good. But he had become my shadow. The faster I moved, the faster he ran.

Behind me I could hear his owner calling, "Wait! Wait!" in her heavy accent. Then it sounded as if she were saying, "My dog charm! My dog charm!"

Geez, I thought. *Calm down and get your dog under control.*

But the owner kept trying to get my attention. She was talking to me in an animated way, but I couldn't understand a word. I turned around and suddenly saw a stream of toilet paper trailing behind me. The Korean lady had been trying to tell me her dog was "chasing the Charmin."

Time stopped.

I thought the toilet paper had stuck to my shoe, and as I reached around to remove it, I discovered, to my horror, that my skirt was tucked up into my panty hose and that I'd been flashing everyone on the mezzanine level and probably a few people in the lobby as well. I yanked off the toilet paper streamer and ran to the safety of my office. I howled with laughter for the next ten minutes as I described to my assistant, Wendy, what had happened. I never wore that skirt again, but I've hung on to it because every time I look at it I instantly Lighten Up.

LIGHTEN UP

Lightening Up (especially on yourself) shifts the intensity and opens a new way of operating that catapults you into the Power Zone.

When you laugh, you release endorphins and chemically alter your physical state. Laughter shifts your energy from low to high. When you're busy, driven, multitasking and moving fast, feeling as if you can't keep up with all there is to do, you are probably in the Fear Zone, a physical place of stress where you're using low-energy choices. Snap out of it! Get over yourself! Lighten Up.

WHY CHANGE?

Lightening Up is the expressway to making higher-energy choices. Laughter enables you to break away from the intensity and drama of a situation. It stops the low-energy spin-offs you are creating. It helps you get clarity and perspective and gives you a break. It helps you instantly go to neutral because you disengage from everything else. And when you're operating at that high a level, it's contagious. It's amazing how people respond when you're playful and in the moment. They pick up on the vibes and lack of judgment and intensity. It's a very welcoming space.

Regardless of the situation, you can always choose how you respond, and nearly any situation can become more bearable if you connect to the humor instead of only to the sadness or stress. If all else fails, and you've tried the other high-energy choices and you're still in a fog — because some days are like that — try Lightening Up. I am not referring to polite, quiet giggles. I am talking about genuine laughter where your whole body shakes and your eyes tear up.

Perhaps you're asking yourself, Does the idea of shifting the energy with laughter also apply in times of sadness or grief? Absolutely, but you must Suspend Judgment about how things "should" be. Mary and Joan's mother died after a long illness. Both the girls and their father were exhausted and sleep deprived when they arrived at the funeral home to make arrangements. As they stood at the front door, Mary said, "If they are playing organ music, I'm going to lose it." The door opened, and sure enough — organ music. Mary tittered, and Joan held her breath, but she was shaking with laughter as well. "Girls, get a grip," their father whispered. The funeral director was a walking stereotype — hushed and somber. As they walked down the hall, Mary and Joan avoided eye contact with one another so they wouldn't laugh.

When they got into the office, they filled out the paperwork, and then the director asked not for their mother's maiden name, but for their mother's *mother's* maiden name. Mary, Joan, and their dad all said different names. That was it. All three of them began giggling. The funeral director looked mortified, which made them laugh even harder. All three agreed that their mother would have laughed the loudest! Their ability to Lighten Up gave them a brief but important break from their pain and grief.

THE OLD WAY OF DOING

If you are like most people, you probably let the momentum and intensity of a situation carry you into the Black Hole. Once you realize you're in it, you employ some variations of trying to stay in control, trying to make a plan to come out of it. You lose your job. You make a plan. *I'm going to do X, Y, and Z. I'll call a recruiter. I'll get my résumé together. I'll get out and network.* But Lightening Up is a lot less work and a lot more fun.

But usually we take life way too seriously. For this next story, I want you to think of a time when there was nothing you wanted more than to make a good impression, and you will understand the mind-set I was in. Once, just after I had started a new job, my staff and I had to take over a meeting that had already been scheduled in a resort city in Mexico. I wanted to make a good first impression, and every detail needed to be perfect. I had a huge amount of information to cover during the premeeting with the executives and had reviewed all the logistical details with my team.

They had scheduled a midmorning break, requesting coffee and fruit. As the break time neared, I expected the hotel staff to discreetly begin setting up. Instead, we suddenly heard the crash of cymbals, the door flew open, and a man in a gorilla suit burst into the room and began passing out bananas.

We were not amused.

I, for one, was furious. I had been clear that I wanted fruit on the break. That didn't mean I wanted a gorilla handing out bananas. Everyone looked at me as if to say, *What is this? What kind of meeting are you running?*

Rather than seizing the opportunity to make light of the situation and have fun with it, I politely escorted the gorilla out of the room. Since he spoke no English and I spoke very little Spanish, we relied on hand signals to communicate, which made him seem like even more of a gorilla. When I returned, I apologized for what had happened. If there was ever a time in my career to Lighten Up and laugh, it would have been then. But I just couldn't do it. I was too terrified that they thought I was an imbecile for scheduling this, and I lost a precious opportunity to connect with my colleagues that day.

THE NEW WAY OF BEING

One place where people could Lighten Up a little more is at the airport. Being a frequent flyer, I am always struck by how serious and stressed out people become with airport delays. One time, my flight was cancelled and I was standing in a long line at Heathrow Airport in London with other passengers trying to get onto the next flight. An American man at the head of the line was berating the poor agent. His verbal abuse became so extreme that the rest of us felt uncomfortable even witnessing it.

A British gentleman quietly made his way between the man and the agent and said, "Excuse me. I am a member of the politeness police, and on behalf of all the people in this line, I am giving you a citation!" The American turned around, glanced at the rest of us, and slowly began to smile. "I'm so sorry. I'm trying to get home for my son's graduation," he said. And he apologized again.

Nearly any situation can use some Lightening Up, but making this choice is easier said than done for many of us. You may find it helpful to refer to these specific steps:

1. Laugh at yourself.

Create a space between you and all the intensity you are experiencing. Absolute presence is the key. Become the observer. Describe the situation as if you were a reporter on *60 Minutes* or your favorite news program. The very act of describing the situation can bring in some lightness that ultimately leads to laughter.

My colleague Ben always seems to fall asleep on takeoff. One time he fell into a deep sleep very fast and was awakened by a terrible noise, which turned out to be *him*, snoring. Plus, he was drooling…just a little. Everyone was looking in his direction. There was nowhere to hide. He immediately coughed, as if that would fool anyone. Since that didn't work, and all eyes were upon him, he blurted out, "Well, clearly, I'm not afraid of flying!"

PLAYING THE FIELD

Think of a stressful situation you are experiencing
   right now.
How might you separate from it?

2. Let your triggers be your guide.

You can Lighten Up faster if you know what's keeping you connected to the intense emotions. Let your triggers be your guide. When life feels especially uncomfortable, tell your-self to Lighten Up. One of my friends, who's very introspec-tive and has done a fair amount of personal-growth work, often announces to people who know her well: "I feel angry because this isn't perfect, and if I don't do it perfectly, my father will leave again, and then I'll die." The ridiculousness of the words, which accurately describe her triggers, always breaks the tension for her.

PLAYING THE FIELD

What sorts of situations trigger you?
How might you Lighten Up the next time you encounter them?
What would it sound like to hear an observer describe these situations in exaggerated terms?

3. Do whatever reliably helps you Lighten Up.

What helps you Lighten Up? It might be golfing, listening to or playing music, exercising, dancing, doing yoga, paint-ing, or being around small children. Have you ever noticed how young children laugh more than anyone else? They can be a great role model for us. Perhaps the activity that helps you Lighten Up is singing, seeing movies, or gardening. For me, it is doing exercise that's intense enough that I'm forced to get into my body and out of my head. I also have a special tape I made of my favorite songs that instantly transforms me. Lightening Up doesn't have to involve laughter. A subtler shift such as those described above can also make the difference.

Also, remember that you don't need to feel totally stressed before you try to Lighten Up! Do it whenever you can, even if things are going well. Figure out what helps shift you. Enjoy all this freed-up energy. If you've become scattered, Lightening Up can restore you to wholeness — even if you're maxed out, like my friend Melanie.

Melanie was a young up-and-comer who felt trapped in her job. She wanted to leave but felt she couldn't for financial reasons. Each day seemed more stressful than the last. To top it off, she got food poisoning on a trip abroad that wouldn't go away and had to collect stool samples and ship them in an express UPS package right away.

Melanie didn't know when she'd have time to find a UPS station and then remembered: "My company uses UPS!" As she walked into the mail room with her package of samples, the irony of the situation was not lost on her. She had a big smile on her face the rest of the day and was definitely Lightening Up.

But the joke was also on Melanie. She had always noticed the nice-looking single man who lived in the house behind her. She was in her backyard one Saturday when he stopped by and said, "I noticed your house is for sale." She offered him a tour, and as they walked through her home, they casually determined one another's availability. Things were going well until they got into the kitchen. She filled a glass of water for him, and when she turned around she realized, much to her horror, that he was looking down on the table at the envelope marked URGENT! STOOL SAMPLE RESULTS containing words like *bacteria* and *infection*. Suffice it to say, he never called her. In fact, the tour came to an abrupt halt, and he excused himself. She never saw him again. Ever. Melanie still laughs about this.

PLAYING THE FIELD

Describe a time when laughter dramatically shifted a situation.

What makes you laugh?

Which activities reliably help you Lighten Up?

To master this high-energy choice, become as graceful as you can at Lightening Up, even under the most difficult of circumstances. While in South Africa I heard Bishop Desmond Tutu speak. At the end of his incredibly moving speech about the enormous challenges the country faces, one of my colleagues asked, "How do you cope with all of the human suffering?" His answer was, "Find the humor. Find a way to laugh. It lightens your spirit and paves the way to hope."

HAMMERING IT HOME

Several years ago, during one of the busiest times of my career, I was relocated to Dallas and decided to put down some roots and to build my own home. I selected some builders who prided themselves on "one-stop shopping."

Things became pretty hectic. One delay turned into another, and one week before the final walk-through, there were still all sorts of loose ends. The builder looked me in the eye and said, "I give you my word that we will have this work done in the next week." So we wrote up the "punch list" with details about the work that needed completing. Six months later, the items on my punch list had not been touched. I was livid.

The head office told me not to feel bad because unlike some customers, "at least, little lady, you're living in your own home."

I made a judgment that they wouldn't take me seriously unless I got tough. The next day I set aside an entire morning so I could write a detailed letter to the *president* of the company. I took great pains to list every problem and every conversation in chronological order. When I finished the letter, I signed not only my name, but also my title, "regional vice president," and my company name. I thought the title would give me more credibility. I concluded with a list of the jobs I expected to have done by the end of the week. I stressed that I needed caulking in the bathtub, in the kitchen, and especially in the laundry room. They hadn't done the job properly, making water damage in those areas more likely.

Two days later I was about to leave for work when I heard the doorbell ring. There stood a man from the construction company with a big smile on his face.

"Hi ma'am, my name is Jim, and the president personally sent me over to take care of your needs. We are sorry you have had so much trouble."

You could have knocked me over with a feather. I asked him if he needed the list, and he said he had his own copy. I said, "Super. I will be back at the end of the day. Let's meet at 5:00 and go over everything." To my surprise he responded, "No problem, ma'am."

I gave myself a congratulatory pat on the back during my drive to work. *See, Brenda? All it took was getting tough and going to the top.*

That evening as I entered my subdivision, I got several nods and waves from some of the men working in the neighborhood. Again, I complimented myself. I finally had their respect. Jim and I sat down and went over the list, and he showed me that all the work had indeed been completed.

As I was signing off on the list, Jim said, "Ya know, Miss Brenda, you seem like a nice lady. May I suggest to you that the next time you need caulking in the bathtub, that you do not spell it c-o-c-k-i-n-g?"

I could have died on the spot.

I felt my face start to turn the first of many shades of scarlet. I was so humiliated! How could this happen? I had been so frustrated for the past six months. The builders had patronized me and made me feel stupid for simply wanting the job completed. Well, now the job was completed, and I still felt stupid and patronized. All I could think of was how I made such a big deal of "needing cocking in the bathtub, and the kitchen, and especially in the laundry room."

Suddenly I began to smile, and then I started to laugh. As my laughter increased, my humiliation decreased. Jim could not resist, and he started, too. We were laughing so hard, it took a good five minutes for us to regain our composure. I said, "Jim, you must think I am a total idiot!" He started to grin and said, "Well, I don't, ma'am, but the president put the letter up in his office, and it is creating quite a stir."

I had thought it was my authoritative stance and tone that got all the work to happen, when actually it was a sloppy spellcheck. The laughter shifted the energy from tense and serious to lighthearted and warm. This is a metaphor for life, which is often not fair. I had every right to be upset — and that was only one reality. Another reality was that they had every right to laugh at my typo. I chose the reality of laughter and connecting with Jim. Had I chosen the reality of upset and lingering on injustice, these incidents would still bother me today.

Instead, Jim and I created such a great bond from that experience that the entire time I lived in that house, Jim personally took care of any issues or repairs. Had I stayed entrenched in right and wrong, I would have never created this outcome. Five minutes of laughter put us back into neutral and did more to create a lovely relationship than six months of ultimatums would have.

SUMMARY

- When you laugh, you release endorphins and chemically alter your physical state.

- Laughter shifts your energy out of the Fear Zone and into the Power Zone.

- Laughter helps you instantly go to neutral because you disengage from everything else.

- Create a space between you and all the intensity you are experiencing. Become the observer. Absolute presence is the key.

- Let your triggers be your guide. You can Lighten Up faster if you know what's keeping you connected to the intense emotions.

- Engage in whatever reliably helps you Lighten Up. It might be listening to or playing music, exercising, dancing, doing yoga, painting, or being around small children. Perhaps it's singing or seeing movies or doing housework or gardening.

CHAPTER NINE

TUNE IN

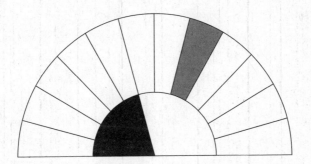

Have you been run over on the information super-highway? Do you go around in a techno trance, alternating among your cell phone, Blackberry, and computer as you dash to your next appointment? Have you forgotten how to focus on the human being in front of you? This chapter will help you Tune In and focus on what's happening right here, right now.

Most problems today stem from living in a state of disconnection, and most disconnection is caused by people feeling so rushed that they don't pay attention. Or maybe they're so invested in their agenda, they can't take in another perspective without skewing it. When you Tune In, you stop and get present. We all lead hectic lives, and this is not very easy to do, as you will see from the story below.

I had just come off seven eighteen-hour days at a conference in Miami filled with nonstop people, activities, and crises. I'd scheduled a two-day date on the weekend with my own bed. No phones. No Blackberries. No walkie-talkies. No people. Just sleep. Can you relate? But my plans changed at the last minute, and I was flying out to the Dominican Republic to meet then-president Hipólito Mejía.

My client was considering an educational event in the Dominican Republic, and the government hadn't yet confirmed its financial support. One of our colleagues had a high-level contact who had arranged a meeting. How do you say no to a president? My neighbor sent my passport on the last flight out of Chicago so I could leave Miami the next morning. Our evening gala ended at 1:00 a.m., and I left for the airport at 4:00 a.m.

When we arrived, two government officials greeted my colleagues and me. We climbed into the official Mercedes, where two more people, including an extraordinarily intimidating general, joined us. All I could think was, *Where am I? What's the agenda? Who's attending? I'm hungry, and I must look like hell.* Hours later, our bodyguards took us to a restaurant, and just as the food arrived, everyone's beeper sounded. The general jumped up and ran out.

"*¡Ahora!*" (Now!) they shouted, pulling us up from our seats and running us down the sidewalk alongside the building toward the street. I glanced longingly at my receding meal. Alerted by the commotion, the president's bodyguards began running toward us, then retreated when they saw the general. The crowds parted like the Red Sea, and el Presidente emerged. News cameras flashed at the *gringa* in the middle of the pack.

I strained to remember, *Is it one kiss or two in this country?* I couldn't recall. Normally I would have researched this and have learned a couple of lines in the language. The president greeted me in Spanish and leaned in for the kiss. I planted a big one. I was a little awkward, not knowing which cheek to go for, and left a huge red lipstick mark on his cheek.

Then he asked me something in Spanish. Clearly, he thought I understood him. Everything began to move in slow motion. There was absolute silence. All the cameras and microphones zeroed in on me, as did Presidente Mejía.

I Tuned In and enthusiastically replied, "*¡Sí!*"

That appeared to be the right answer. The president smiled and swept down the stairs to his car. As it turned out, he had asked, "Are you having a wonderful time in our country?" They sent us to the airport in the president's flag-festooned car with a police escort and sirens. Because I had Tuned In, I was able to override physical exhaustion and mental stress, and I actually had enjoyed myself. Tuning In helped me transcend cultural differences and enabled me to fully participate.

TUNE IN

It's time to unplug from the wired world and focus on the human being in front of you right now.

When you Tune In, you optimize all your senses, including your sixth sense. You miss these valuable insights when your mind is in the past or future. When you Tune In, you become more open — not guarded, not protective, not on the attack, not trying to figure out what to do next. This requires a great deal of concentration, particularly when you bounce from one activity to the next. You start noticing how your boss interacts with others and what works best. You get a sense of your child's state of mind before she even says a word. You instinctively say the right thing to your friends. When you Tune In, you interact better with everyone in your life because you understand what matters to them.

WHY CHANGE?

Nearly everyone has heard that we tap into only 10 percent of our brainpower. Tuning In, however, enables you to override physical limitations and emotional obstacles and tap into the other 90 percent. It also reduces stress. You access new possibilities when you don't have any agenda other than being present to what's happening in the moment. This enables you to connect with others on an intangible, but nevertheless very real, level.

Before I met Presidente Mejía, I had spent an hour with the minister of tourism. As is customary in Latin American countries, this involved loads of people, including his two assistants, my two colleagues, and a translator. The minister, his two assistants, and five other women, including the minister's wife, came in and out of the room. They all spoke Spanish. Typically in these situations the translator becomes the focus, but I kept my complete focus on the minister with the intention of connecting with him, insisting silently that he look at me, and he did, throughout. He maintained eye contact, and even though I didn't know what he was saying, I could pick up the odd word and follow him enough to compose appropriate follow-up questions. The bottom line was that we all understood the issues at hand and the next steps to be taken. For the first time in six months we were all on the same page.

People feel it when you're completely and unequivocally focused on them.

Tuning In is a high-energy choice that aids communication and breaks down barriers, moving you out of the mundane, monotonous details and bringing you to a place where big things can happen easily and quickly.

THE OLD WAY OF DOING

Before I learned to Tune In, it was all too easy to fall into the Fear Zone of the Energy Spectrum. In the situation described above, I would have felt I could not contribute in an all-Spanish meeting, that I'd been set up to fail with no prep time, that I couldn't have any impact without a translator. Or I might have given up, feeling that I had absolutely no ability to influence the situation. This limited thinking would have dropped me in the Fear Zone, totally disempowering me.

I would have prepared for, anticipated, and researched to ready myself for these meetings. But on this trip I didn't have a chance to check on anything. Instead I was reminded to Tune In and was able to override physical exhaustion, hunger, crabbiness, and language barriers to accomplish my mission. With the president, I would have turned and said, "Would someone please translate?" And I would have skipped the kisses if I weren't certain of the exact number. But even when you mess up, as I did somewhat with the lipstick smear, if you're Tuned In, it doesn't matter because you're fully present and have established a bond with another human being.

When we don't Tune In, we're living in an altered reality that can feed misunderstandings and misconceptions. We all have a warped, one-sided view of life. We spend so much of our life not Tuning In because we're always thinking about the next thing, solving the next problem, anticipating what will happen, or reliving and rehashing the past. We're day-dreaming about the vacation we just took and how much fun it was. While on vacation we're thinking how much we dread going back to work. We're thinking about what our child should do next, even as she is trying to get our attention right now. It takes conscious effort to Tune In. It doesn't feel natural because we spend so much of our time mentally and physically orbiting from place to place.

We drift away so easily for two reasons. First, we're trained from a young age to multitask, and that can be useful — if we're giving our full focus to each item that comes across our perceptual screen. Second, our society is oriented around sound bites. Advertisers count on short attention spans. You and I are not wired to get present and focus. Think about when you're in a new relationship or have just met someone. You don't always Tune In because you're thinking about how you're coming across and wondering if you sound stupid. You think you're enhancing the connection, but all you're doing is disengaging and disconnecting. When you check out, you miss in-the-moment opportunities.

For example, if you want to broach an important topic like

having another child or moving a parent into a retirement home, you might wait for the "right moment" to bring this up with family members who will be involved. But do you stop before you speak and actually get present to everyone who's in the room? Think of all the managers you've worked for who run from one crisis to another, or your pressure-prompted co-workers who get everything done in the eleventh hour. Or the friend who's a blur of activity and crisis. They're wired into that way of working and living. Once you get into that pattern, it's hard to get out. Any behavior that's driven by fear or desire is low energy and ultimately more stressful, because you're on a path to the Fear Zone. Tuning In reduces stress and keeps us connected to the Power Zone. If you're not Tuned In, you're leaking energy. We often Tune In when under duress. Events like a performance review, a medical emergency, or a death in the family force us to engage.

THE NEW WAY OF BEING

Why Tune In? Because it's the optimal way to operate. When you're tuned out, you daydream, worry, and drift into low-energy choices. You become less effective because you're not focused and using your energy optimally. Tuning In requires that you shut out all the stimulation and chatter and focus on who and what are present right here, right now. This is a learned skill, especially when something is going on in your life that feels bigger than anything else, like a health scare or a death in the family. Here's how to make this important choice a way of life:

1. Start small.

You are undertaking a major behavior change, so begin with incremental steps. At home, get clear about your key priorities, like being completely present as you tuck your kids into bed. At work, select the activities that will get your full attention. Do this even in face-to-face meetings, Tuning In on the most important topics. At first you may feel exhausted trying to be mindful every second. Pick the nonnegotiables and grant yourself room to move in and out when other issues are up. It's all about leveraging your energy.

There will always be pressing issues vying for your mental energy. The reason you take quantum leaps when you Tune In is that what's in front of you often has a gift to offer, if you just stay present long enough to see it.

PLAYING THE FIELD

When have you Tuned In successfully? What happened?
Do you know someone who Tunes In automatically?
What is it like interacting with this person?

2. Be in the now.

We jump from home to work to email to voice mail to in-person meetings. Our brain chemistry changes, and different parts of us are triggered, depending on what neural pathways we are using. We actually develop stronger physical links in our brain to the areas of life to which we consistently Tune In than to those we don't pay attention to. You're emotionally wired in. If you've had a tendency to Tune In to the Fear Zone and want to shift instead to high-energy choices, you will actually be overriding a physical connection as you rewire your neural network.

One way to begin making this behavioral and brain chemistry change is to do something to break up what you're doing. Have a drink of water, take a walk, go to the restroom. Or at least acknowledge that you're working from a different part of your brain and don't have your full resources at your disposal. Because you don't. Our senses, emotions, and intuition allow us to take in volumes of information that email and voice mail simply can't. It *is* the thought that counts. Even if you never master this choice, do your best. Tune In on something that would normally trigger you, and choose not to react. Pick a situation that is especially emotional, that triggers anger or frustration. If you set a goal to Tune In three times a day (e.g., with your child, in a team meeting, and with your spouse) you will get significant practice. Don't let emotional triggers be the only reminders to Tune In.

I refined my ability to Tune In when I took some improv courses. To be great at improv, all you need to do is focus precisely on what you're doing that second. It absolutely forces you to be completely in the now. The next line you speak is contingent on what is happening. Part of what's so exciting about improv is that it's unpredictable. You don't know which way to go. Plus, when you're in the moment you're human and you goof, which is often endearing to the audience. The really talented people don't stand there thinking of what to say next. They are completely in the moment, and the lines just fly out of their mouths.

During one class, the director called a man and a woman on stage and set the scene: "You're in the bathroom. You're getting ready in the morning together, and you're in front of two sinks, facing the audience. You're working on synchronicity and timing. You need the audience to understand your relationship. And you can only say one line total between the two of you."

Allyson got up there with Dan, a good-looking man she didn't know, and felt a little intimidated to be doing such an intimate scene with a complete stranger. He walked in, and she followed. As Allyson came around the corner, he pulled her into his arms and slapped her on the butt. They then faced the mirror (which was the audience), brushing their hair and flossing in sync. Then, as she turned to walk out, she paused, turned, and popped her head back in, saying, "By the way, what was your name again?"

The line got a big reaction from other students. Not being a one-night-stand kind of gal, Allyson felt uncomfortable in this setting, and yet, because she had stayed present, the perfect line had emerged. She and Dan polished the scene and used it in their final performance, which brought the house down. Two local critics said that their scene was the best of the show.

PLAYING THE FIELD

In the past, when would it have benefited you to Tune In with your family? At work? With friends?
In which situations at home or work will you begin to Tune In?

3. Realize that sometimes all you need to do is notice.

Noticing shifts the energy and makes room for a different outcome. You don't always have to have the answer. When you've Tuned In, you feel present, calm, detached, and alert. When you tune out, you feel distracted, spacey, and not particularly connected to others. You may have your own cues about these two states. When I tune out, I feel disconnected and out of sorts, and when I Tune In, I immediately feel focused and curious.

When another person makes the effort to Tune In to me, I feel energized, appreciated, and heard. Think about the doctors and dentists you've particularly liked. It's probably because they looked you in the eye and saw you as a person, not as a diagnosis. Do the same for the people you love most. Whenever you've been apart from your child or spouse, take a moment to Tune In before getting into conversation. This is especially important at the end of the day. The person arriving last may need some time to decompress, either alone or by sharing her day. The person who's been home all day may need a break. The child may need some love. Take the time to notice. Tune In and find out.

A colleague once told me about a Carnegie Mellon study showing that spending two hours on the Internet per week can alter your brain chemistry (including levels of endorphins and estrogen). You go on autopilot and start operating like a machine because you're not interacting with humans: *What's the task? Get it done. Do it fast. What's next?* We lose our warmth, our personality, and our perspective, and we become predisposed, without making a conscious shift, to being less than our best with other people. In other words, we forget to notice. Have you ever been working on your home computer, and when your child or spouse walks in to talk to you, you look at them as if to say, *Go away! I'd prefer to look at my email?* We have more challenges Tuning In than ever before. You can use cues like the ringing of your phone to stop, get present, and get human before even saying "Hello."

PLAYING THE FIELD

What is a typical situation in which you forget to Tune In? How can you prompt yourself to Tune In better during those situations?

TUNING IN FROM THE HEART

One busy morning, Jane, a manager in a large Los Angeles firm, met with her assistant, Kenisha, to discuss a critical customer issue. "Look, we are very busy. We really blew it with this customer. Here's what we need to do to fix it. Let's go."

To Jane's surprise, Kenisha resisted her direction. In fact, she seemed critical and short-tempered. Just before her meeting with Kenisha, Jane had been triaging 150 emails and a full voice-mail box so she could deal with several minor client emergencies. She hadn't encountered anyone live in the past two hours. Her first exchange with Kenisha failed miserably, because she was still in a "techno trance." *This will work. Check it off the list.* Her words sounded harsh, and her emphasis came out completely wrong. Not surprisingly, Kenisha held her position and dug her heels in even further.

The more disagreeable Jane seemed, the more disagreeable Kenisha became. Kenisha didn't tend to be short-tempered, so when she became emotional, Jane knew something was going on. She stopped and Tuned In. She pushed herself back from the desk and looked at Kenisha. That's when Jane noticed how pale she looked. And how scared. For the first time, Jane noticed Kenisha's closed body language; her arms and legs were crossed, and she was turned away. That's when Jane made a real connection with her assistant. It rewired her brain chemistry, and she moved back into real human interaction.

Jane stopped trying to control Kenisha and began asking her general questions to encourage her participation in the conversation, but that seemed to bring out even more negativity. They were getting nowhere. Finally, Jane said, "Kenisha, please tell me what is happening here. You do not seem like yourself, and I'm concerned." Kenisha disclosed that she had just returned from the doctor, where she had had a series of mammograms. She felt worried about the results and had also reacted badly to the procedure. She had a metallic taste in her mouth, and her whole body felt agitated.

Once Jane connected with Kenisha on a human level, the conversation became much more civilized; they were communicating, listening, and working out the problem. With their connection reestablished, they were able to take care of the issue at hand, and Jane learned a valuable lesson. Moments like these connect us to the Power Zone, move everyone to a higher level of operating, and accomplish what we want more quickly.

SUMMARY

- It's time to unplug from the wired world and focus on the human being in front of you right now.

- Most problems today stem from living in a state of disconnection, and most disconnection is caused by people feeling so rushed that they don't pay attention.

- When you Tune In, you optimize all your senses, including your sixth sense.

- You access new possibilities when you don't have any agenda other than being present to what's happening in the moment.

- Start small. You are going through a major behavior change, so begin with incremental steps and Tune In when it's most important at home and at work.

- Be in the now. If you set a goal to Tune In three times a day (e.g., with your child, in a team meeting, or with your spouse) this will provide significant practice.

- Notice what it feels like to be Tuned In and tuned out. When you've Tuned In, you feel present, calm, detached, and alert. When you tune out, you feel distracted, spacey, and not particularly connected with others.

CHAPTER TEN

SCAN

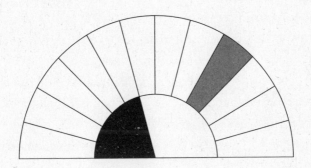

Do you know people who seem to have a natural ability to connect with people, no matter where they go? Who can walk into a party, family gathering, or meeting and instantly get the lay of the land? They naturally know who needs attention, who's disengaged, who's on top of the world, and who's grumpy. They are automatic Scanners. How do they do this? For some it's a learned skill. Others acquire it in childhood, which is how it happened for me.

"Hold still!" the mean nurse snapped. She gripped my arm more tightly and turned it, hell-bent on finding a tiny vein that would cooperate. Every opportunity she had to admonish me about something, she did. She'd already yelled at me twice. I felt annoyed at being back in the hospital. I was ten, and my asthma had been under control for several years. I did not want to be back here getting poked by doctors and nurses. What I didn't know was that the sore heel I'd complained about for the past two months was actually osteomyelitis (poisoning of the bone marrow). I was facing a two-week stay at the hospital and the possible loss of my right foot. The asthma drill I knew. This was different. I needed massive doses of antibiotics, and I needed them two weeks ago.

My arms were throbbing so much I felt I couldn't take it. My eyes started to tear up. The other nurse was really nice to me, and I especially didn't want to upset her. She and the nasty nurse had attempted twelve times to insert an IV drip and still hadn't succeeded. I could tell that neither of them was going to do it right because they were both tense when they walked into the room. The mean one was overwhelmed from an emergency, and the nice one was horrified at how swollen my arms had become and didn't want to make another attempt to pierce them. Dr. Bryant, who had delivered me, had been angrily yelling at them in the hall. When he came in, he turned his back to me and addressed them quietly: "It's an IV drip, for God's sake. You're putting her in jeopardy. Get it done!"

The kind nurse intervened. "Who else is on shift right now? We need someone who's fresh." She left and returned a few minutes later with a male nurse — a rarity back then — but what stood out even more was the upbeat energy this man brought into that dreary room.

He stood at the doorway with his hands on his hips. His eyes said it all. They twinkled with calm confidence as he focused completely on me. "Well, hi! My name is Mark. It sounds as if you haven't been having any fun. Let's take a look and see what we have to work with." Everyone else had gone straight for my arm. Mark connected with me first, putting his hand on my head and caressing it. His confidence seeped into me. He smiled warmly and took my hands into his huge ones, then turned them over.

"Oh, my! Haven't we made a human pincushion out of you! This just can't be any fun for you."

He was talking *to* me. The nurses and doctors had talked *about* me, as if I weren't there. His sweetness allowed me to express my feelings without being afraid.

"Yes. It's not fun."

"Well, let's make it fun then. Let's place a bet that I can do this in two tries. Anyone want to make this bet with me?" he asked, looking around at the three of us.

"You pick the arm, Brenda. Which one hurts less?"

I handed him my left one, beginning to play the game.

"Which vein wants to come out to play?" he sang (and he couldn't carry a tune, which was very funny to me). I almost laughed and looked to see if one of my veins would actually volunteer.

He got it on the first try.

I'd known he would succeed the second he walked into the room.

SCAN

When you Scan, you move into a detached state of observation, using all your senses to take in the physical, emotional, and intuitive information in your environment.

Whereas when Tuning In you focus on an individual, when Scanning you perform a quick sweep of your whole environment, taking in information without attaching to it. In other words, you Tune In to the micro, while you Scan the macro. Even though you're engaged as you Scan, you're not trying to control or direct an outcome. Your whole job is just to notice. It's almost a form of meditation and creates the same type of calmness. Knowing you don't have to *do*, that you just have to observe, can feel like a relief when you're in a tight spot.

That's what Mark did. He cut straight to the problem at hand: I was scared to death, and my arms ached. He knew he had a job to do, but he knew he couldn't do it without connecting with me first. His Scan took about three seconds. Then he used the information he had gathered to change the energy from fear to play. I connected with him and cooperated with him because I felt acknowledged. My body had been shutting down because it hurt and because I was afraid. His light touch relaxed me, enabled me to open up, and pulled me out of the Fear Zone so that he could help me.

I had learned to Scan as a child. It was a way to pass time in the hospital, a sport. I would watch someone and Scan them to figure out his or her life story. Then I would validate it when the person spoke. I had no idea I was practicing and honing a skill that would serve me my whole life.

Mothers tend to be incredible Scanners. They take in so much so quickly, and they intuitively know what to do next. One summer Nina, the neighborhood babysitter, was watching five of us while our parents were at work. We swore she had eyes in the back of her head. The second we thought of something we weren't supposed to do, she was on to us. How could she keep control of so many of us? She was a great Scanner.

If you have kids, you've probably noticed that children also seem to be born with this ability. They take in everything, picking up on nonverbal clues that adults don't. They can sense a change in the environment because they notice all the details. They know which of their friends is having a hard time at home. They know whether this is a good moment to ask for an increase in their allowance or to go out with friends. Children are like human barometers. They can pick up on subtle changes in their parents' interactions often before the adults acknowledge them. They haven't yet created filters or learned *not* to Scan. They see through the veils and cut to the heart of the matter, which sometimes exhausts their parents.

Before babies can speak, they learn to read the people around them, and often their behavior reflects the unspoken feelings in the room. When manners and protocol become important, they are weaned away from this ability. Also, as we grow older and learn how the world works, in most of our daily activities we focus on ourselves rather than on others. But there are exceptions. Think of a boss you've had who motivated you well because he understood you. Chances are he was a great Scanner. Although women get credit for having more intuition about people and things, Scanning is not gender specific. It just has to do with how well you pay attention.

WHY CHANGE?

Scanning gives us a great reality check. If you're like many people, you spend most of the day inside your head. When you stop and consciously Scan, you can take in even large amounts of information more quickly to better assess how to approach a situation. Scanning uncovers valuable clues about the people in the room. You can be much more effective both at home and at work, because you'll pick up on what others don't. Because I was in and out of the hospital so frequently, Scanning was the way I took in the truth when I was so ill and so young that adults felt I couldn't handle it. Once I was in the hospital, I could tell by their pace which nurses were happy, which were sad, who was glad to be at work, who wasn't, and if they'd keep me in the oxygen tent any longer.

Often it's what you don't know that will help you the most, and your openness allows you to access the Power Zone, where anything can come in. When you take the time to Scan, you create connections that help you communicate more effectively. You don't Scan to manipulate, but to gather information. The only motive is to see the truth and observe it for what it is so you can become more sensitive, more aware, and more equipped to handle any situation. Scanning makes you more effective in any setting. That's different from manipulating to get what you want. If you Scan for your own gain, you'll get busted.

Salespeople are great Scanners, and the best ones don't make assumptions ahead of time. They don't assume that when a couple enters the appliance department that it's always the woman who does the laundry. Great Scanners make their pitch to both people. The next time you deal with a salesperson, ask yourself: Was she very helpful? Did you end up getting more than you expected? Did the clerk seem to read your mind? The next time you socialize with a friend, Scan before you start your conversation. The next time you find yourself in a tense situation, Scan the people in the room. What you might find beneath the surface will help you make an authentic connection. You may discover that the person who seemed to want to control things is actually just stressed out, or that the person who seems "fine" is actually not feeling fine at all.

With Scanning, life becomes richer. All the high-energy choices help us tap into the Power Zone, but Scanning opens up the world around you on a different level — an intuitive one. I travel all over the world, and Scanning is a big part of how I take in information about other cultures. It's also how I find good bargains when I shop. And it can show up in small ways, like when I discovered a robin's nest camouflaged perfectly above my back porch. If you Scan, you're open to the unexpected. It opens the way for incredible experiences to unfold.

THE OLD WAY OF DOING

It's so easy to go into autopilot and to stay there. As adults, the closest most of us have come to Scanning is observing closely in order to manipulate an outcome. You Scan your spouse or children before making an important request. You bond with the receptionist at work to find out what's going on or with a prospective customer by noticing and remarking on something in his or her environment. You comment on the photo of the receptionist's kids or on the prospective's alma mater, or you share some area you have in common. This is a form of Scanning, but if you do it to manipulate, it will backfire. The second others suspect you're not being authentic, they become suspicious. People sense when they're being used. Even if they don't pick up on it consciously, your attachment to an outcome creates a kind of static in the Field that people pick up on. This will not inspire teams to carry you through the tough times or motivate your spouse or children to do what you want. Bonds formed this way don't last.

THE NEW WAY OF BEING

Although your actions may appear the same, your inner shift into Scanning will create all sorts of new opportunities. Here's how to do it:

1. Detach from your agendas.

If you're Scanning for personal gain, you'll skew your data and your results. If you Scan for the truth, you won't. You must let go on some level. You can't invest your emotions in the results or have any goal, other than to learn the truth.

Jerry and Carol tell the story of going to watch their son, Brian, in his second year of soccer. Jerry was cheering him on and encouraging him to try harder. He couldn't understand why Brian was doing so poorly. Carol did a Scan and noticed that Brian was not responding and didn't look as if he were having any fun. He wasn't smiling and appeared to have no connection to the other kids on the field. He barely listened to his coach's suggestions.

On the way home in the car, Carol simply asked him, "Sam, do you like playing soccer? Do you want to do this?" After a long pause, during which Carol shot Jerry the *don't you dare talk* look, Brian answered, "No, not really. I just joined because my friends did." Jerry realized that he had been more attached to his agenda of Brian becoming an athlete than he was to noticing what his son wanted. He immediately made a course correction on the road to being a great parent.

PLAYING THE FIELD

Give an example of when you were able to detach from your agenda and learn something significant while Scanning.

What kinds of agendas at work interfere with your ability to Scan?

What kinds of agendas at home interfere?

---

2. Go into "notice" mode.

When we observe we receive gifts, even if we don't see them right away. Make it a habit to step back and Scan. Remove your filters and judgments and take in what's happening. You sample this state of mind when you Suspend Judgment, discussed in chapter 7. Simply become an observer. The pieces of information will start coming together like a story unfolding before you. The more open you are, the more clearly the meaning will come through. If, on the other hand, your Head Trips are so loud that they're drowning out everything else, this won't happen. So hush up! Let the meaning wash over you. Try not to draw conclusions (premature evaluations) too quickly. Don't let your Head Trip become the reality you create.

The moment you notice your stress level rising, become the observer. Do this even when things seem to be going well.

You might be surprised at what you learn. Scan when you drop off or pick up your child at day care. Scan when you first walk into a meeting. Scan as you sit down in your favorite restaurant. When in doubt, Scan. As you do, some information will be very clear. Some will be clearer later after you've had some time to absorb. If you have a hunch about something, set it gently aside and see what else comes through.

Scan during situations in which you don't tend to observe or even make eye contact. You may be pleasantly surprised. Yesterday the Windy City was particularly windy, and as my colleague Rick got into an elevator, he noticed how disheveled all the passengers looked. "Nice hair day," he remarked. Everyone smiled and began talking about their adventures in the wind. He complimented one of the women on her coat and learned about a winter coat sale that was happening at one of his favorite stores. Everyone seemed to leave the elevator happier than when they had entered it.

Scanning is one of the most practical everyday choices because it gives you so much information. The key is to be emotionally detached. If you Scan while you're having a bad day, it may not be as effective because everything may be colored by your depleted state and susceptible to misinterpretation. Your hunches are going to be affected, and you won't necessarily realize this. Rick happens to be losing his hair. If he'd been in a low-energy place that windy day, he might have entered the elevator thinking, *Everyone has so much hair, except for me. I look terrible. Everyone is staring. The wind probably flipped my comb-over, and I don't dare check.* Needless to say, he probably would not have added anything to everyone's day.

Your low-energy choices can drown out everything else when you're in a low state of mind. Part of the wisdom of this choice is to know yourself well enough to recognize when you're projecting a depleted state onto the day. You may need someone to help you sort out what's real and what's not. When you're in a low-energy place, remember what a difference a day makes. Scan the same things again tomorrow, and you may see a whole different scenario.

PLAYING THE FIELD

Describe a time when your emotions clouded your ability to Scan.
What happened? Describe the outcome.

BORING THE BOARD

After he had spent two months in a new assignment as an executive director for an association, Tom realized that his group needed to make some big changes in order to survive. This first board meeting would set the stage. He worried about this meeting on the entire flight from New York to Paris, even though Ingrid, the president, was completely in sync with his plan. Needless to say, Tom wanted to make a good impression on the nineteen people from seven countries who'd be sitting around the table.

The next day at the meeting, Ingrid was nervous and ignored their carefully planned agenda, bringing up the very changes they'd agreed not to discuss. Tom was floored and immediately felt the defensive shift in the room. As he

Scanned the group, he noticed folded arms and lack of eye contact. Some members were expressionless. He felt a huge disconnect and rising anger. The quieter the board got, the more emphatic Ingrid became. The tension kept building, and whispered side conversations erupted in a half dozen accents. She was losing them.

Tom had to let go of his upset and his judgment that Ingrid had made a big mistake and instead focus on salvaging the meeting. He interrupted, saying, "I sense that you all need more context and data before you can consider making such sweeping changes."

He had nailed it.

Suddenly the tension dissolved, and all the board members leaned forward and nodded. Tom earned their respect by conducting a Scan and naming the energy in the room instead of pushing what they weren't ready to hear. The group was then open to moving on to the next items without bringing their discomfort to the rest of the agenda. Several people later told him how well he defused the situation, paving the way for the very changes he wanted to make.

SUMMARY

- When you Tune In, you focus on one person. When you Scan you take in your whole environment.

- When you Scan you move into a detached state of observation, using all your senses to take in the physical, emotional, and intuitive information in your environment.

- When you Scan, you perform a quick sweep of your surroundings, taking in information without attaching to it.

- Scanning gives you a great reality check. When you stop and consciously Scan, you can take in even large amounts of information more quickly to better assess how to approach a situation.

- You can be much more effective both at home and at work because you'll pick up on what others don't.

- As adults, the closest we come to Scanning is observing closely in order to manipulate an outcome.

- When you Scan, you need to detach from your agendas.

- If you Scan for personal gain, you'll skew your data and your results.

- Go into "notice" mode. Remove your filters and judgments and take in what's happening.

- Remember that if you Scan while you're in the Black Hole, your hunches are going to be colored by your low state of mind.

- As you Scan, some information will be very clear. Some you'll have to set aside for the moment.

CHAPTER ELEVEN

TAP THE TRUTH

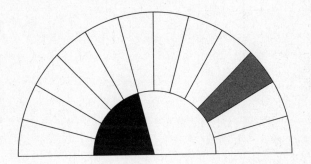

Do you ever tell "white lies" to protect someone you love — or yourself? Do you sometimes go along with something because you feel you have no choice? Are you afraid to tell your boss what she doesn't want to hear? This chapter will give you the tools to Tap the Truth, regardless of your circumstances. Let me tell you about how I faced a particularly tough situation and how the truth truly did set me free.

Our newest client had put me in a tough spot. The contract negotiations with Mark, our COO, had been so contentious that they didn't want him involved in our first project together. I had worked hard to earn their trust. For six months I had been on the road every week, and we were finally at a place where I felt I wasn't under daily attack. And now this. The last thing I wanted to do was ignore this request. I also didn't want to stir things up with Mark, who happened to be my boss.

Mark was very bright and knew the business better than anyone. But he could be volatile. Like many COOs, he wanted to have control. Most of my colleagues were afraid of him. It was not uncommon for people to call Mark's assistant before a meeting to find out what kind of mood he was in so they could plan their approach.

I felt absolutely trapped. How could I possibly handle this in a way that met everyone's needs? I started Head Tripping, playing out every possible scenario and their mostly disastrous outcomes. I considered finding a believable reason for Mark to disengage from the account. I could make it about *me* by telling him, "I feel the need to do this solo." That wouldn't work because going solo had never been an issue. In fact, Mark wanted to be involved because I already had too much influence with this client, and if I left the firm this could negatively affect the relationship.

Perhaps I could go back to the client and tell them, "Work with me on this. Mark will be involved, but I will manage him to make sure your needs are met." I knew what an energy drain it would be, trying to stay one step ahead of Mark, and I felt tired just thinking about it. In desperation, I actually considered ignoring the whole thing and hoping it would go away. And then a new idea emerged:

What if I told Mark the truth?

He would probably become confrontational and demand to call the client and ask them what was going on. He would then pour all his energy into making the client like him again, at the expense of my entire team and me. *How could I let that happen, when we've worked so hard? My review is coming up, and if I'm on Mark's bad side, what will happen to my increase? And how will this affect future assignments? The last time I tried to tell Mark something he did not want to hear, he became annoyed, dismissive, and unsupportive. There's too much at risk: the client, the relationship with Mark, my future.*

All these Head Trips were exacting a toll. They were disrupting my sleep, and I became irritable and preoccupied. I was getting headaches, finding little comfort in my Comfort Zones, feeling disoriented from going in Loops, and was about to create the mother of all Magnets. I decided I had to take the leap and Tap the Truth, not knowing what the outcome would be.

When Mark and I met, my palms were clammy. I concentrated on just relating the client's request without having to come up with the answer. My objective was to communicate the message clearly and to focus on that, rather than on possible outcomes. I kept peeling away extraneous thoughts or agendas and let the truth stand by itself:

"This is awkward for me, but the client has asked that you not be involved in this project."

It was extremely hard to stop talking at that point because my natural inclination was to try to rescue him, to defend the client's intention, or to diminish the impact so Mark wouldn't get mad. The dialogue that followed wasn't easy or comfortable for either of us. Mark became defensive. I again stated what the client wanted, without putting my own spin on it, without getting all wound up in what he said. I didn't match his emotional pitch. I stayed detached, took a deep breath, and kept Tapping the Truth.

My palms were sweating. My heart was racing. But I stayed still because it was the right place to be to solve the problem. I continued to listen to what Mark was saying and let him know he was heard, without taking a position. When Mark diffused all his highly charged emotion, he began to ask questions I could answer. Remarkably, we were able to come to an agreement that met everyone's needs — all because I'd stepped out of the Fear Zone and into the Power Zone by Tapping the Truth.

TAP THE TRUTH

You tap your greatest power when you live in integrity with yourself and with everyone else.

When you Tap the Truth you stay connected to your real power. Try Tapping the Truth, then hanging out in the unknown, or what I call "working the Gap." Do not attempt to shape an outcome. This can feel difficult for people with empathetic personalities — especially women. But this is the portal through which another outcome can emerge. If you move out of the Gap too quickly, you don't allow for this innovative process. My remarkable outcome with Mark would not have happened if I'd sugarcoated the situation, held back, or told a half-truth.

If you're like most people you may be skeptical. *Surely you can't say everything you think all the time.* The art of Tapping the Truth lies in your intention and choice of words. If a friend asks how you like their new home, instead of saying, "I hate it!" you can truthfully say, "It's not my style, but I can tell you're really happy here." If your partner asks if her new dress makes her look fat, you can say, "To me it's not as flattering as your blue one." In an argument with a sibling, instead of hollering, "I can't stand you!" say, "I'm so uncomfortable and feel so angry right now." When you catch your child in a lie, don't call him a liar. Say, "Something doesn't add up" or, "I feel confused." Focus on telling your own truth, and be sure not to impose it on the other person.

WHY CHANGE?

When you Tap the Truth, positive energy flows, and higher-energy solutions seem to appear as if by magic. You have self-respect, and you feel respected by others. This sense of well-being becomes contagious, and you accomplish your goals more easily. Do your best to live and work as much of the time as you can in that space between the truth and the outcome where breakthroughs occur. Otherwise, you will be doomed to a life of groupthink, which generates low-energy choices and can lead to the Black Hole. Though sometimes scary, Tapping the Truth is ultimately less work because you don't have to remember what you've told to whom. You'll also have fewer messes to clean up and apologies to make. Without all these detours, life becomes simpler and you move forward faster. You feel lighter and happier.

Although that lightness and happiness don't always come right away, you will always be on solid ground when you Tap the Truth.

THE OLD WAY OF DOING

If the benefits are so clear, why don't people Tap the Truth more often? Most of us grew up buying into the most common myths about the danger of Tapping the Truth. How many of these beliefs still run your life?

1. A half-truth is better than nothing.

2. I won't get what I want.

3. The other person can't handle the truth.

4. Someone's feelings will be hurt.

5. If I ignore the problem long enough, it will go away.

6. I will lose my relationship/friend.

7. People will be out to "get me" if I say what I really believe.

8. Confrontation serves no purpose and will make things worse by stirring up emotions.

9. It's okay to tell white lies.

10. It's not my responsibility.

These top-ten myths share one critically important component: *fear.* We tell half-truths and white lies because we fear getting in trouble, disappointing someone, or being rejected. If we don't get the sale or if we lose a customer, we fear failure. If our boss hears the whole truth, we might lose credibility, and he might yell at us or fire us. We fear losing someone's loyalty or friendship if we hurt her feelings. What if she gets mad and tries to get even in some way? We ignore problems because we fear our inability to solve them. Often the confrontation we most fear is with ourselves and our perceived shortcomings. When I was wondering how to take Mark off that client project, I put myself through those mental dramas because I was afraid. That feeling drowned out my inner voice, and I allowed it to throw me off-balance. Fear pulls you out of the truth faster than anything else.

And, as we learned about Magnets in chapter 6, fear can be very toxic because it feeds on insecurities and produces low-energy choices. It's also extremely contagious. Bad news spreads fast, whether it involves work-related rumors like budget cuts and layoffs or world events, like natural disasters and terrorist attacks. Most of us collude in the spread of fear every day because we tend to share the negative much faster (and with far more people) than the positive. In fact, if you pause and notice the next five conversations you have, whether you are talking with family or friends or eavesdropping at the local 7-Eleven, you may find that most people are complaining, blaming, or worrying aloud.

With the Internet, bad news travels faster than ever. Unhappy customers (and employees are internal customers) who complain in the anonymity of a chat room potentially influence thousands of other customers. This negativity in turn affects employee turnover, client satisfaction, and the bottom line.

When you create bonds based on negativity and fear rather than on the truth, those bonds don't hold. Contracts and verbal agreements based on honesty last longer. When you act out of fear, your thoughts, feelings, words, and actions easily become disconnected from your values and from the person you aspire to be.

THE NEW WAY OF BEING

To Tap the Truth consistently, follow these steps. Most of these behaviors are invisible. They happen inside us. But the results are evident to everyone:

1. Find the courage to commit to the truth.

It takes courage to Tap the Truth all the time, and it often takes courage to listen. People have always struggled with this. Most of us seem to want some form of external validation before stepping forward. Einstein originally recanted his theory of relativity (e = mc²) because it was so radical, and he only came forward with it in 1905 after a colleague pressured and encouraged him. In his autobiography, Einstein said one of the greatest regrets of his life was that he didn't put forth this theory sooner.

It takes a leap of faith to step out alone with a new idea when you don't know how it will be received. Do you want to operate out of the Fear Zone or the Power Zone? Do you want to be limited by what others think instead of operating from your own unlimited potential? When you don't Tap the Truth, you bounce all over the Fear Zone, from one drama to the next.

PLAYING THE FIELD

How much time do you spend in Head Trips about Tapping the Truth?

Can you recall a time when although it took courage to Tap the Truth, you experienced some remarkably positive results?

2. Make sure your thoughts, feelings, words, and actions are consistent with who you are.

It's easy to slide out of Tapping the Truth — an embellished fact here, an omission there. Before you know it, the ideas in your mind, the emotions in your heart, the sensations in your body, the sentences coming out of your mouth, and the specific steps you take don't line up. Then you have to direct most of your energy into maintaining all these inconsistencies, creating a powerful energy drain. Make sure all these aspects of your life reflect one another. Having integrity is a moment-by-moment decision, and it's often difficult, especially when you have to make tough choices that directly affect people's lives. No matter what the situation, you *can* stay true to your values.

Henry Givray, president and CEO of SmithBucklin, the world's largest association management company, re-joined the firm in 2002 to lead the company through some significant changes. The previous four years, the company had gone through a challenging ownership change. It was a critical point in the company's future, and some difficult choices faced him. His theme from the beginning was "It's all about the people." When asked if there were to be layoffs, Henry Tapped the Truth, saying, "I sure hope not, but if it does happen, I guarantee we'll do our best to minimize it." True to his word, he kept the layoffs to a minimum. In fact, the company has recently gone through an ESOP (employee stock ownership plan), and the employees now own 100 percent of the company. Henry was Tapping the Truth when he said, "It's all about the people." What better way to show that than by letting the people own the company?

PLAYING THE FIELD

*In what areas of life do you say one thing but do
    another?*
When that happens, how do you notice it?
In what ways do others notice this incongruity?

3. Tap the Truth because it is the right thing to do, not because
you want to get something from it.

When we choose to do things for the right reasons, opportunities emerge that we couldn't have imagined. No matter
how well intentioned it may be, any attempt to manage or
manipulate the outcome undermines this power.

Sometimes the truth is that you don't know the answer,
and your power comes from acknowledging that. A colleague
of mine named Jon had a harrowing experience with an
employee named Diane. Fortunately, Diane had insisted on a
ninety-day contract to make sure they were a fit, because she
almost immediately alienated most of Jon's staff. She made
constant demands that Jon didn't agree with and, within her
first month, demanded that a longtime administrative assistant
be fired.

Jon learned that Diane had sued her former employer for
wrongful termination and wasn't sure what to do. He dreaded
going into work each morning and counted the days as he
rode out Diane's contract. One afternoon, while driving back
from a client presentation, Diane told Jon in outrage that her
demands hadn't been met. Jon wanted to Tap the Truth and
also felt there was no way Diane could hear that she was
the main problem. When they arrived at the office, he parked

the car, turned to Diane, took a breath, looked her in the eye, and said, "Diane, I don't know what to say." It was a moment of absolute honesty. Jon wished he had more to offer, but he just didn't.

"Well, something had better happen!" Diane shouted as she exited, slamming the car door.

An hour later, Diane came into Jon's office clutching an official-looking document and asked if she could have a few minutes. Jon felt a rush of fear, then took a breath and said, "Sure. Come in." Diane closed the door but did not sit down. Jon tried not to flinch.

Diane began: "I just want you to know that you are the first boss who really listened to me," she said, with tears in her eyes. Jon was stunned. He'd felt inadequate not knowing what to say earlier, but because he'd Tapped the Truth, she'd felt heard. After that meeting, Diane settled down, finished out her contract, and left the company on good terms. Jon never found out what the paper was that Diane had in her hand when she'd come into his office, but to his relief it wasn't a summons, as he had initially thought. His most troublesome employee challenge got resolved because he listened first, then gave an honest reaction. Diane called him several times during the next year to stay in touch and to thank him again for being such a caring boss.

PLAYING THE FIELD

Think of a difficult truth you have to tell. What words can you use that will let you own it without imposing it on the other person?

4. Stay detached from the outcome.

In a goal-oriented world, where we have a tight vision of the end result, Tapping the Truth may not seem to make any sense. More often than not, though, the outcomes we create by Tapping the Truth are better than anything we could have achieved by force.

When Diane slammed Jon's car door, he imagined all sorts of possible scenarios — none of which felt very good. When he took his attention off the end result (even a positive one), he was able to tap the power of integrity because he was willing to feel the discomfort of the Gap and to allow higher outcomes to emerge.

This isn't to say that you don't have to prepare when you are dealing with troublesome situations. Do your homework. Be at the top of your game. Know your options. But don't get so locked into any of them that you snuff out the possibility of a better solution. When you detach from the outcome, you're less likely to get sucked into the vortex of Head Trips or the downward spiral of Loops. You'll think more clearly and be able to recognize a higher-energy solution as it emerges.

Once you select one course of action, you eliminate other possibilities. And a course based on someone's *possible* reaction is a house of cards built on speculation, not reality. When Jon decided to Tap the Truth with Diane, he had to set aside any inclination to influence her reaction. If he had thought about how to manage her reaction, he would have leaked energy and stepped out of his power. When he lay aside all agendas, the situation resolved itself. He surrendered to Tapping the Truth. This is the only way to do business, and the only way to live.

5. Listen when others Tap the Truth.

Sometimes you need to listen while others Tap the Truth before you can tell your own. One of the masters of this art is Roger Tondeur, CEO of MCI Group SA, the prominent pan-European association, communications, and events management group. Roger's full attention is always on the present moment. Whether he is talking to one of his vice presidents or to the receptionist, his ability to listen and to retain conversations is incredible. He is not attached to ego or status; he's focused on connecting, always seeking other viewpoints. Roger knows as much about some people he's had one dinner with as I do about some of my relatives. When I asked him how he does that, he said, "Because I'm honestly interested in what others have to say." That's probably the key to Roger's (and his firm's) success.

6. When you slip out of Tapping the Truth, get back in as fast as you can.

Once you've surrendered to the idea of working the Gap and operating from integrity, the challenge is to stay there. Good people slip out of Tapping the Truth all the time. But you can slip back in at any moment. When you understand the power behind your thoughts, feelings, words, and actions, you can create an environment based on integrity, and your life will move forward in a way it never has before.

To get back into Tapping the Truth, ask yourself three questions: Where am I out of alignment? Where am I not being authentic? What part of this is not me? You must choose to give your authenticity more energy than fear. When you have integrity, you tap into your real power.

PLAYING THE FIELD

Have you slipped out of Tapping the Truth? What will you do to rectify this?

7. Honor who you are.

Tapping the Truth means accepting yourself as you truly are. My mother was very good at keeping up the appearance that we had more than we did. Her mother had done the same. At a very early age, if I would sneeze too loudly in church, or if my sock had a visible hole in it, she would say, "Now, don't be a Pogson." I didn't realize until I was older that *Pogson* wasn't a real word but actually referred to a somewhat un-sophisticated family in the small English village where my grandmother lived. Over the years, the townspeople became accustomed to the Pogsons behaving somewhat inappropriately in public. In our family, being a "Pogson" meant being a little left of center, not being enough, not keeping up, yet it was a term of endearment. My cousins and I still yell, "Pogson alert!" and break out laughing when one of us does something that doesn't quite fit the image we try to convey, like splurging on a new pair of extravagant shoes but then planning our whole day around the first matinee movie time to save a few dollars. Embrace the Pogson inside you.

My friend Cathy grew up on a tobacco farm and worked the fields. Even though she's a successful executive now and earns a six-figure income, she still buys her household items at K-Mart and looks for sales. She also cleans her own house. It's not that she's cheap. Doing these things keeps her in tune with who she is. When you lose sight of who you are and give up too many aspects that are central to your core, you are not living with integrity and are less able to Tap the Truth.

The more you live with integrity, the more you incorporate all the aspects of yourself. All your multiple realities are true, but if you focus on only one, you have less to work with. For example, say you are a father, a son, a husband, a brother, an employee, a friend, and a Little League coach. One truth is that you're getting a divorce. Another is that your job is going great. Another is that you are supporting your elderly parent, and yet another is that you're estranged from your son and only see him at baseball practice.

If you live with only one of those realities, *I'm a bad father*, you're limiting yourself, because you are many other things, and your power comes in telling the truth about all your realities. You're a good father. You're a great employee.

And the more you are able to see all these truths, the easier it is to accept all your realities and live with them every day, because that's when you're most powerful. The ultimate truth lies in embracing all the multiple realities that are you. When that happens, you move through a magical portal and into the Power Zone on the Energy Spectrum.

PLAYING THE FIELD

List all the multiple realities you are living in right now.
Which one is getting your focus?
How can you embrace the Pogson within you?
Have you tried to suppress any aspect of yourself in order to impress others?

TAPPING THE TRUTH, NO MATTER WHAT

Over time, we live in multiple realities with our parents. First, we are the cared for, and then we become the caretakers. It is easy to have the perception that when our parents are elderly, we can't tell them the truth because they've been telling us what to do our whole lives and it just doesn't feel natural. One of the most difficult situations many adults face is when they start making decisions for their parents, especially when the changes they're recommending are not what their parents want.

My sisters and I were becoming increasingly concerned about Dad's driving. We decided to be direct rather than talk around the issue. When we met, I said, "Dad, we've noticed that your reflexes aren't the same, and it's not your fault. You're eighty-six years old, and we don't think it's safe for you to drive anymore." I added that I'd been with him a couple of times when I'd noticed his slower reactions. He hated hearing it.

"Honey, I've been driving for seventy years," he answered. To him, giving up driving felt like dying. We talked some more, and he agreed to limit his driving to within two miles of home and to only drive during the day. Six months later, he made the decision on his own to give up driving altogether.

A year later, Dad was hospitalized with pneumonia. When I flew in to see him, I was startled at the change in him. My two sisters see him much more frequently and could not have noticed what was so clear to me since my visit months earlier. He looked very tired and had lost weight. He had fallen, and it wasn't until my sisters and I compared notes that we realized these were not isolated instances. It was time. Dad had to move into a facility where he'd have more support, but he didn't want to move.

What were we going to do? Acquiesce and leave him vulnerable? Pick a place and tell him there were no options? Hire a nurse and burn through his savings? If you've been there, you know how hard this situation can be. *He* had always been the adult, directing our lives. Now we were directing his, and it felt uncomfortable and strange.

We visited him in the hospital and took the direct route once again. "Dad, you can't live on your own recovering from pneumonia. You are too weak. You need nursing care. You need help getting out of bed, bathing, cooking, and making sure you're taking the right medications."

He didn't like it, but he heard the truth. Instead of trying to con him by saying, "This place is really nice. Wouldn't you love to live here?" we said, "You can't stay on your own. We've looked at places and narrowed it down to two. Let's take a look." He really didn't like the idea of moving, so we told him that if he got better, he could move back into his condo and that we wouldn't sell it. If he liked it in the new place, then we'd sell it. We were honest, and we gave him options. Dad was shocked that we were taking control, but I think he was even more shocked that the three of us girls had actually agreed on something.

Dad moved from the hospital directly into a senior community. Because he was so motivated to go back to being independent, after only one month he moved from assisted care to independent care and told us, "Sell the condo." Three months later, he was the happiest he's been in five years. He can go to the cafeteria and have three meals a day and has put on fifteen pounds. And his social life has expanded exponentially. We wish we had told him our truth five years ago, when he wanted to buy the condo. Why hadn't we? We were afraid we would hurt his feelings and make things more difficult for him.

Tell the truth, regardless of the circumstance. We always seem to anticipate that the other person's reaction is going to be worse than it usually is. When you Tap the Truth, you leave room for miracles.

SUMMARY

- When you commit to Tapping the Truth and you let go of the outcome, you are able to move through the heaviness of a situation and to access wisdom, no matter how difficult the circumstances are.

- You are not Tapping the Truth when you hide your feelings about something while insisting that everything is fine. When you step out of integrity you create static, which other people sense.

- The top-ten myths about Tapping the Truth (which are all fueled by fear) include:

    1. A half-truth is better than nothing.

    2. I won't get what I want.

    3. The other person can't handle the truth.

    4. Someone's feelings will be hurt.

    5. If I ignore the problem long enough, it will go away.

    6. I will lose the relationship/friend.

    7. People will be out to "get me" if I say what I really believe.

    8. Confrontation serves no purpose and will make things worse by stirring up emotions.

    9. It's okay to tell white lies.

    10. It's not my responsibility.

- Find the courage to commit to Tapping the Truth.

- Make sure your thoughts, feelings, words, and actions are consistent with who you are.

- Tap the Truth because it is the right thing to do, not because you want something from it.

- Stay detached from the outcome.

- When you slip out of Tapping the Truth, get back in as fast as you can.

- Sometimes you need to listen while others speak the truth before you can tell your own.

- Honor who you are.

CHAPTER TWELVE

BELIEVE

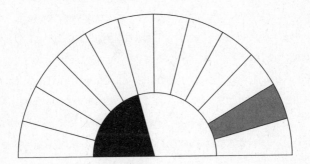

Can you think of a time when you believed so strongly in something or someone that others believed in it, too? Can you recall an instance when you had so much conviction that those around you were moved and inspired? This is the power of Believing. You can generate portals of possibility, no matter what reality you are focused on.

Have you ever tried to lose weight? If so, imagine yourself in my place as you read about this magical experience: "Oh, my God. This can't be right." A few women in the locker room glanced over and smiled. I stepped off the scale, and started again, moving the little weights around until the bars balanced. Wow! It said the same thing. I'd lost eleven pounds since my last weigh-in at Weight Watchers. Add that to the seventeen I'd already lost...that meant I'd lost a total of twenty-eight pounds! I was in shock and had not one, but two, different women test out the scale. Both declared it accurate.

I was beside myself. Twenty-eight pounds! I hadn't been so slender since high school when I'd starved myself. It had been five weeks since I last weighed myself. Clearly, the combination of the Weight Watchers program and my workouts had paid off. I was pretty darned pleased with myself and was grinning from ear to ear. I had fun getting dressed, suddenly realizing how loose everything felt. As I left the gym and walked to the office, I caught a glimpse of my reflection in a glass building. Normally, I would quickly turn the other way, but today I looked right at my reflection and thought, *Looking good, twenty-eight pounds, oh yeah!* As I strutted past the building I noticed a few men do a double take. I thought to myself, *twenty-eight pounds, oh yeah!* and smiled right back.

As I entered my building and got in the elevator, one of my colleagues said, "Brenda, you look great. Have you lost weight?"

I said, "Why, yes, I have lost twenty-eight pounds. Thanks for noticing!"

I was on a high. My feet didn't feel as if they were touching the ground. Everything went right that day. It was perfect. I easily closed two difficult negotiations, and when I thought it could not get any better, I got a call from not one, but two, old boyfriends. I was feeling so good, I thought, *I'll go weigh in at Weight Watchers to validate my victory. I want to get my ribbon that shows I am within five pounds of my goal weight.*

I marched into the meeting confident and relaxed as I

handed my booklet to Margie, who asked me to hop on the scale. I cheerfully complied. Margie handed me my booklet, and to my surprise, she'd written one pound instead of eleven. I smiled and said, "Excuse me, Margie, you forgot a one." She looked at the booklet and said, "No, honey, that's right. You lost one pound."

Huh? Surely there must be a mistake.

"Margie, I know for a fact I've lost eleven pounds since my last visit, totaling twenty-eight!"

Margie looked over her glasses, sized me up, and said, "Okay, get back on the scale."

I stepped on one more time. She quietly said, "Geez, honey, you've only lost one pound."

One measly pound? How could that be?

I self-consciously slithered off the scale. I don't remember a thing anyone said because I was too caught up in Head Trips and Loops. By the time I got home, I felt awful. I just sat down on my couch and stared at my walls.

I took a few deep breaths, and all of a sudden, I got it. Because I'd believed I'd lost twenty-eight pounds, all day I had acted like it, convincing others, all because I completely, unequivocally, down-to-my-bones believed it. This high level of energy was contagious and spread to everyone with whom I came into contact. This is the power that's available when you Believe.

BELIEVE

What you deeply, authentically believe, you create.

The immediate and powerful positive results I enjoyed while under the spell of my false belief about weight loss underscore the potential you tap when you view your life or job through the lens of *unequivocal* belief. Technically, I had not lost twenty-eight pounds, but because I authentically believed I had, the quantum field mirrored back that reality. Was I deluded? Yes! Did it matter? No, because I believed it with every fiber of my being. Do not confuse this with positive self-talk or trying to will it or convince yourself. Every morning when you get up, you have a choice about how to create your day. Why not choose to Believe? I recently heard about an interview with his Holiness the Dalai Lama in which he was asked how he remained so positive in spite of all of the insurmountable challenges he and his people faced. He simply and quietly replied, "It feels better."

When you choose to Believe, you tap into the Power Zone, where things move more easily. When your intention and belief are that strong, you have no fear, so you don't make low-energy choices, and you accomplish what you want not only consciously but also subconsciously. One of my realities is the critical voice in my head that always wants me to lose weight. Once I had the proof that I'd lost weight (when the two women in the gym confirmed that the scale was accurate), I truly Believed it and created one of the best red-letter days of my life. I left no room for any other option. I was able to access the Power Zone from a very pure place. There was no static, no distraction. Just a pure stream of knowing.

Instead of fear I felt exhilaration and joy, which are very high-energy emotions, as are love and appreciation. Even though I was operating on incorrect data, the reason it made me feel so good was that I Believed it down to my soul. You've no doubt experienced this too, perhaps when an adult believed in you as a child or when you've been swept away by a powerful idea or political or social movement. My friend Nick, for example, always Believed he would have children. He married in his midforties and a week after returning from his honeymoon was diagnosed with a very aggressive form of cancer. His wife, Laura, became pregnant, and Nick absolutely, unequivocally believed he would beat his illness and live to see his daughter. And he did. Zoe was born on April 11 — Nick's birthday. Six months later, both of them are happy and thriving.

WHY CHANGE?

Who wouldn't want to more easily create what they desire? If you allow for the possibility, you can create outcomes in your life you didn't think possible. Believe you can make some real and substantial differences because you're not tethered by what family, friends, co-workers, bosses, or the culture at large think. You're freeing yourself. You're no longer dissipating your energy by responding to what everyone else expects from you. You step into your true power. And when enough people adopt this powerful frame of mind, they can change an entire nation — or even the world.

THE OLD WAY OF DOING

The old way of doing has been just that — doing. We have devoted ourselves to doing things that address the one reality we are focused on at that time. These separate realities may have included positive self-talk, visualizing, or willing things to happen — whatever we think is the answer. Throughout the ages, many of us have used different ways to transcend our low-energy aspects. Tried-and-true approaches have included particular ideologies, religions, or spiritual practices, including meditation, yoga, and intuition. We've journaled, chanted, and attended support groups and silent retreats. Some of us have gone on vegan diets and had colonics. Our homes may be rearranged in perfect accordance with the precepts of feng shui. We've experienced flashes of transcendence, and when we haven't sustained that state of nirvana, we've felt discouraged and disappointed in ourselves.

The reason these approaches don't fully allow us to maintain that level of bliss is because they represent just a few of our realities. The key to the new way is not trying to force a state of happiness and joy all the time. Instead, it's about accepting the many aspects of who we are by not rejecting or minimizing them. We live multiple realities at all times, and when we Believe, we get to play in the full power of the quantum field.

Don't get sidetracked by subjecting the lower-energy parts of you to a self-help program. Your job is not to reform them. They operate at too low a frequency on the Energy Spectrum to ever be transformed. Remember, no matter how nice you are to a Komodo dragon, he will still eat you. It's why he exists. The same is true of your lower-energy aspects. They will always be with you. Their purpose is to operate at that frequency in your life. Rather than trying to change them, your job is to learn to live with them and to acknowledge the role they play and how they affect your choices. You created these to serve you, and when you were younger or in crisis, they have. But at some point they stop working. You arrive at a crossroads. You can keep re-creating the same circumstances, or you can break free to realize your dreams. The gift of your low-energy aspects is a brand-new life. Just because you recognize this, does not mean they will go away. When you see they are at work, you can make higher-energy choices. Then you are free.

THE NEW WAY OF BEING

The new way consists not of "doing" but of "being," being and living what you Believe. To achieve this state of mind takes three steps:

1. Recognize where you are on the Energy Spectrum.

Use the chapters in this book as a guide. Name the choice you are making in each moment. As you work more with the Energy Spectrum, you will experience more and more how fluid it is, and you will move in and out of the various choices instantaneously. Knowing when you're in the Fear Zone and when you're in the Power Zone will enable you to stop creating realities you don't want. You will notice that the more you work with the Energy Spectrum, the more three-dimensional it feels. When you view it from this perspective, you will better understand how you can so quickly move from one choice to another. In the beginning of chapter 2 I described the crazy morning I was having when I was trying to get out of town. By being aware of how I was using my choices and that I was in the Fear Zone, I was able to redirect a day that almost felt unsalvageable by making Power Zone choices instead. This is the promise of the quantum field: you can accomplish so much more with absolutely no need for force.

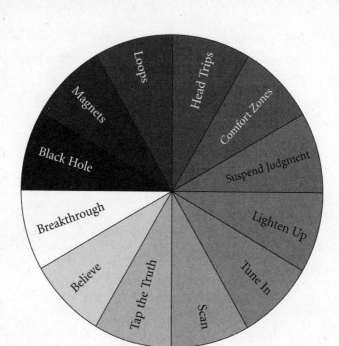

Think of a day when you've been all over the Energy Spectrum. You're feeling sad about the past, trying to control the future, and grappling with the challenge at hand. You've jumped from Tuning In during a great phone conversation with a friend to taking disciplinary action at work that caused a Head Trip, to Lightening Up at the memory of something your toddler did this morning. The key is knowing where you are at any given moment. Your power will come from understanding this, not in trying to control where you're going.

2. Remember that your present reality is not the only, or the whole, reality.

Invite in something bigger than your present reality. The way to work with your multiple realities is to accept, acknowledge, and notice that they've been at work. When you notice, the magic happens. When you can say, for example, "I'm a committed parent, a neglectful daughter, somewhat out of shape, and miserable money manager," you are instantly deposited at the Power Zone of the Energy Spectrum. The transcendence happens when you accept all that you are.

If you garden, you probably become obsessed with the weeds. No matter how often you pull them out, they always come back. Our low-energy choices are like that. You can spend all your time and energy getting annoyed that they are ruining your life; you can try to prevent them or get rid of them. The answer is to acknowledge them, bless them, and appreciate them. Without your doing a thing, they just appear on their own and self-propagate. They're hardy and show us how to survive.

In a similar way, we need to acknowledge how our low-energy choices have operated in our life. Without our low-energy aspects, we cannot experience the Power Zone of the Energy Spectrum. We would not be whole people without them. Why aspire to a permanently weed-free patch? It's just not going to happen. And remember that many weeds bloom and can actually be quite beautiful.

My friend Erin Caldwell, cofounder of Vancouver-based Quantum Ties Inc., lives in all her realities every day. She also loves to garden. Erin no longer obsesses with the weeds. She views them as a metaphor for the low-energy realities in her life. Learn to love your Comfort Zones, accept your Loops, and affectionately watch yourself when you Head Trip. When you create a Magnet, face it without fear or despair, and see it as an opportunity to accept a very powerful part of yourself. Here is how she expresses this in an excerpt from her book of poems, *Weeds, Wildflowers and Wonder*:

If I only gather
All that is
Within me
Into my embrace

I spill out over the world
Like fruitful seed
Bringing all to blossom

Please believe me
When I say
The weeds and the wildflowers
Are the true wonder
They hold up your earth
In their darkness and their light
And in loving them
Your heaven comes home[1]

Without your low-energy aspects, you cannot come into your full power, just as you cannot always distinguish weeds from wildflowers. Without exploring all your aspects, and fully embracing all that is within you, you won't be able to offer your "seeds" to the world, and they will not blossom. The very things you're trying to change, reform, or transcend are actually the seeds to coming into your full power. When you embrace them, "your heaven comes home." In other words, heaven comes to you. You you attract it and you don't have to go get it.

3. Create the space to invite in your highest reality and your wildest dream.

This organic way of living is an invitation to become a quantum citizen, living an interdependent life. You are no longer alone. The quantum field is waiting to welcome you into this new reality. And as you are able to hold all your realities with love, you become a hologram for the larger universe and the larger reality. This way of thinking, though it may seem simple in its essence, can be very tricky to apply. The simplicity is in accepting all the multiple realities of who you are. The difficulty comes when you're in the grip of one of the low-energy choices and that truly appears to be the only reality. Don't let it be.

As David Hawkins reminds us, "There's nothing to feel guilty about and nothing to blame. There's no one to hate, but there are those things that are better avoided, and such blind alleys will become increasingly apparent. Everyone has chosen his own level of consciousness, yet nobody could have done otherwise at any given point in time. We can only get 'there' from 'here.'"[2]

PLAYING THE FIELD

Think of a situation that's got your full attention right now.
Describe two possible low-energy perspectives about this situation.
Describe two high-energy perspectives.
Now think about how your choices have been supporting the low-energy view that has been dominating your thoughts and actions.
How will you create and maintain a high-energy view?

When you play in the quantum field, you raise the bar by raising your frequency. Your interconnectedness with everyone and everything activates the Energy Edge. Barriers dissolve. How do you begin? With your very next choice. Life happens, and difficult things will occur. As a quantum citizen, you can face anything life throws at you, even from the deepest, darkest Black Hole.

PLAYING THE QUANTUM FIELD WITH THE HEART

Even though I was deluded about the weight loss, I created that reality. You can choose to Believe, no matter what reality appears to be happening in your life. My mother and I shared an intuitive connection, and for much of my life I thought she was my link to the quantum field. Her greatest gift to me was showing me that she wasn't. Here's how I learned how to Believe.

My mother has been a powerful influence all my life, so it was confusing and upsetting one Thanksgiving when she wasn't acting like herself. This usually upbeat woman seemed distant from the moment she and Dad arrived on Monday to spend the whole week with me, and she also had a very short attention span. What was going on? I watched her like a hawk and asked about her health. On Wednesday, when she admitted she wasn't feeling well, I made an appointment with a doctor. He said that she had some irregular symptoms, and though he wasn't too concerned she should see her own physician when she returned home.

We celebrated Thanksgiving with my cousin in Wisconsin.

Mom had always been a person in constant motion, and that day she could barely make it from the sofa to the dinner table. Every year, she'd make a big deal of the pecan pie we have for dessert, smacking her lips and rolling her eyes with delight as she takes each bite. This time, she barely spoke and just picked at it. Moments later she was lying down on the sofa again. She looked at me and said, "Something's really wrong."

We called the doctor. He said to check her blood pressure, and when he heard the numbers he said to take her to the emergency room immediately. On the way to the hospital she put her hand on my knee and said, "Honey, I'm dying."

Eight hours later she was diagnosed with leukemia.

My mother, a very youthful sixty-six, who had never been sick, was now gravely ill. I stayed with her at the hospital all that night and the next day, thinking about how I would rearrange my life to be with her as she went through treatment. That night she insisted I go home and get some rest. The next morning I woke up with a migraine and knew something was wrong. As I quickly dressed, the hospital called to say Mom had had an aneurysm and to get there right away.

She was semiconscious when I arrived. Later in the morning, she had a second aneurysm. I stayed in her room that night, trying to make sense of what was happening. On day three the neurosurgeon said we were dangerously close to stabilizing her in a vegetative state and asked if she would want that. As we struggled to have a long-distance family meeting with my sisters and make a decision, the physician stepped into the room and said, "Your mom has taken matters into her own hands. She's just had a third aneurysm."

While my mother lay dying, I was able to be with her, holding her hand and talking to her. Because of the discussions we had had about Dad's health, I knew the last thing Mom wanted was to be hooked up to a machine. We decided to turn off the life support. I felt worried that Dad would drop at any second with a heart attack. My cousin, Dad, and I surrounded Mom. I held her left hand in both of mine.

"Okay, Mom, you can let go now. Don't worry about Dad."

I was aware that the machine was slowly shutting down, but my focus was on my mother. At the moment the life support flatlined, I could feel my mother leaving, and I looked up at the ceiling and said, "I love you, Mommy dearest."

A buzz of energy shot through my left hand and up my arm. It felt like a warm rush of pure love and joy injected into my system and landing straight in my heart. It was the most blissful, serene moment of my life. In that instant, I knew she would be fine. *You've got these gifts, Brenda. Believe. I have been your conduit, but the power is in you. Now go do something with it.*

And so I have.

You will too.

ACKNOWLEDGMENTS

I would like to thank my agent, Roger Jellinek; my editor, Georgia Hughes; and the incredible team at New World Library for believing in this book and making it better.

Special thanks to Winnie Shows for making the words flow on the project "with no end." I would also like to acknowledge Erin Caldwell for steadfast support and generosity of knowledge and spirit. Big hugs and love to my dad for always being there and for never saying "I told you so." Thanks to Laurie — *you are the wind beneath my wings* — Hansen for your friendship, sense of humor, and ability to talk on the phone longer than anyone I know.

Finally, I feel a deep sense of gratitude:

- to Peter Hawley for helping me understand the creative process of writing;

- to my family and friends (you know who you are) for your love, patience, and encouragement;

- to Fred Alan Wolf, PhD, for your thoughtful comments;
- to Mark Combs from Clarins;
- to Nigel Tufnel for making it "one louder";
- to All That Is.

CHAPTER 1. THE FIELD

1. Fred Alan Wolf, *Taking the Quantum Leap: The New Physics for Nonscientists*, rev. ed. (New York: Harper Perennial, 1989), 128.
2. Lynne McTaggart, *The Field: The Quest for the Secret Force in the Universe* (New York: HarperCollins, 2002), xv.
3. Masaru Emoto, *The Hidden Messages in Water* (Hillsboro, OR: Beyond Words Publishing, 2004).
4. David R. Hawkins, *Power vs. Force: The Hidden Determinants of Human Behavior* (Carlsbad, CA: Hay House, 2002), 136.
5. Hawkins, *Power vs. Force*, 196.
6. Hawkins, *Power vs. Force*, 196.
7. Hawkins, *Power vs. Force*, 133.

CHAPTER 3. COMFORT ZONES

1. Anaïs Nin, http://www.brainyquote.com/quotes/authors/a/anais_nin.html.
2. Gay and Kathlyn Hendricks, *Conscious Loving: The Journey to Co-Commitment* (New York: Bantam, 1990), 125.

CHAPTER 4. HEAD TRIPS

1. Candace B. Pert, *Molecules of Emotion: The Science behind Mind-Body Medicine* (New York: Scribner, 1999), 18.
2. Wendell Berry, "The Peace of Wild Things," from *Collected Poems, 1957–1982* (San Francisco: North Point Press, 1985), 69.

CHAPTER 7. SUSPEND JUDGMENT

1. Dr. Marilyn L. Kourilsky, cited in Lance A. K. Secretan, *Reclaiming Higher Ground: Creating Organizations that Inspire the Soul* (self-published, 1997), 50.

CHAPTER 12. BELIEVE

1. Erin Caldwell, from *Weeds, Wildflowers and Wonder*, unpublished.
2. Hawkins, *Power vs. Force*, 127.

and control, need for, 38–40, 54
the Energy Edge, 46–51
Fear Zone, 43–44, 45, 53 (*see also* Black Hole; Comfort Zones; Head Trips; Loops; Magnets)
and good vs. bad days, 29–31, 53
knowing where you are on, 209–10
and low- vs. high-energy choices, 32–33
neutral, power of going to, 45–46, 53
the new way of being, 42–44
the old way of doing, 33–37
overview of, 29–31
Power Zone, 24, 43–44, 45, 53 (*see also* Believing; Breakthrough; Lightening Up; Scanning; Suspending Judgment; Tapping the Truth; Tuning In)
and putting yourself last vs. first, 41, 54
reasons for change, 32–33
summary of, 53–54
and the Triple Threat, 38–41, 54
exhilaration, 206

F
fatigue, anticipatory, 75, 77, 89
fear(s)
as contagious, 189
as corrupting, 76
vs. courage, 50
identifying, 84–85
and Magnets, 111–12, 114, 118–19
of Tapping the Truth, 188–89
Fear Zone, 43–44, 45, 53, 110, 135–36
See also Black Hole; Comfort Zones; Head Trips; Loops; Magnets
feng shui, 208
the Field. *See* quantum field, playing

field, definition of, 6
focusing. *See* Tuning In
Franken, Al, 109
frequencies, high vs. low, 16

G
Galileo, 11
Givray, Henry, 191
good/bad, 29–31, 53, 131
gossip, 77, 78
Greeks, ancient, 11
Groundhog Day, 93–94
grounding, 5

H
Hawkins, David R., 15–16, 136, 213
Head Trips, 73–80
vs. action, 84–85, 90
and angst/stress, managing, 82, 90
anticipatory fatigue caused by, 75, 77, 89
awareness of, 78–80, 89
as conscious, 73–75
definition of, 75
and letting go, 85–87
and love- vs. fear-based action, 78
Magnets created by, 77
and need for control, 43
and neutral, power of going to, 87–89
the new way of being, 78–87
the old way of doing, 77–78
overview of, 24, 73–75
vs. reality checks, 82–84, 90
reason for change, 75–77
sickness caused by, 76, 89
sleep disturbed by, 78
summary of, 89–90
and Suspending Judgment, 85
triggers of, 78, 81, 90
Hendricks, Gay, 68

Brenda Anderson is vice president for global business development for SmithBucklin, the world's largest association management company. She also serves as CEO of the Society of Incentive and Travel Executives (SITE), a global society with members from eighty-two countries. She holds a master of liberal arts degree from the University of Chicago and has been named an honorable professor by Shanghai Normal University. Recently, Brenda became an associate with Quantum Ties Inc. (www.quantumties.com), a consulting company that operates in the Field every day for its clients. She lectures internationally and lives in Chicago. Her email address is Brenda@quantumties.com.